CUSTOMER DEVOTION

CREATE WILDLY PASSIONATE CUSTOMERS TO DRAMATICALLY GROW YOUR BRAND

— **Mike Case** —

The brightest minds in business believe in Customer Devotion

"*Customer Devotion* is a powerful 'must read' for marketers seeking to better understand and further motivate their most valued customers and 'like prospects.' In this compendium of loyalty expertise, Mike shares many strategic guidelines as well as detailed tactics for developing CRM approaches and re-tooling loyalty initiatives across a broad range of industries, including startups and well-established companies. I highly recommend this practical guidebook to marketers focused on creating and benefiting from true customer devotion."

- Rita Bargerhuff Egeland, frm. Chief Marketing Officer, 7-Eleven Inc. and Rent-A-Center Inc.

"Loyal customers are the key to successful brands. Mike Case leverages decades of experience working with a diverse set of start-up, mid-sized and Fortune 500 companies to lay out a road map for the journey of inspiring customers to become, and remain, passionately loyal to consumer brands. Driving brand growth with customer devotion is something every marketer should care about passionately and strive to achieve."

- Scott Emerson, Founder and President - The Emerson Group

"Having worked with him and watched his career from afar, Mike Case fundamentally 'gets' both the head and heart of marketing a brand. He leverages decades of experience grounded in data to masterfully illuminate the path for motivating consumers to become true brand advocates."

- Frank Hamlin, Chief Marketing and Omnichannel Officer, GameStop Corp; fmr. EVP Marketing and e-Commerce, Guitar Center Inc.

"Those who fail to learn from history are doomed to repeat it. Mike does an exceptional job of unpacking the history of loyalty marketing and customer delight in a way that spotlights the valuable lessons you need to succeed. *Customer Devotion* gives you clear insight so that you can avoid making the mistakes of the many who have come before you."

- Angelo Lombardi, fmr. Executive Vice President and Chief Operations Officer, La Quinta Inn & Suites

"For those seeking to fully comprehend the many diverse elements of building lasting customer loyalty, *Customer Devotion* is your answer. Mike Case shares his rare combination of experience in implementing these elements within many industries from the view of both an internal executive and an external consultant."

- Bernie Feiwus, fmr. Chief Executive Officer Neiman Marcus Direct

"As a lifelong marketer I've learned that creating customer loyalty is hard enough, but creating true customer passion is even harder. *Customer Devotion* provides easy to follow approaches to turn your data into powerful insights to drive deep, meaningful customer relationships. If increasing revenue to grow your brand keeps you up at night, *Customer Devotion* should be on your nightstand."

- Paul Frantz, Founding Partner, Ascend Partners; frm. CMO Energy Plus

CONTENTS

Foreword ix

Today's loyalty marketing: Conception 1

Loyalty Strategy Design: Analytics 20

Loyalty Strategy Design: Components 45

Program Implementation 70

Customer Segmentation 86

Retention Begins with Customer Acquisition 107

How to Succeed 127

Epilogue 165

About the Author 167

FOREWORD

Having been there at the launch of what many see as the first real Customer Loyalty program, and having watched how the loyalty practice has evolved, I wish more loyalty practitioners had the benefit of the experience Mike Case and I have had over these many years. While Mike's career with American Airlines started a decade later, we each have participated in the evolution that has led this to become an "Incentive-based Society".

While I was educated as a chemical engineer, a couple of lucky encounters early in my life allowed me to become an early user of the first computers, working at NASA's new Goddard Space Flight Center during college, as an IBM sales trainee after college, and finally as a freshly-minted Harvard Business School graduate launching Epsilon Data Management, a database firm to help organizations automate their membership and donor records.

A decade after launching Epsilon, a Harvard classmate who had just been named American Airlines' CMO asked me to help design the first airline loyalty program, AAdvantage. Using my experience creating constituent relationships, we added the features that helped American engage with millions of its frequent travelers. Later, after serving as Pan Am's Vice President of Sales and Advertising where I launched the first global airline program, and a brief stint as SVP Marketing at Continental

MIKE CASE

Airlines, I launched Brierley & Partners, a marketing agency focused on helping companies design their customer loyalty programs.

Over the next twenty years, working with more than 100 major brands, we recruited and trained many of today's leading loyalty practitioners, welcoming Mike Case from American Airlines early in his career. Over the twenty years since Mike joined Brierley, the loyalty practice has evolved dramatically, with some significant advances, but more than a few changes that negatively challenge the "consumer promise" on which the original programs were launched. Fundamental to the ability to keep this consumer promise is having a program design that rewards consumers in a way that drives sustainable incremental profits for the company.

When I launched Brierley many years ago, if I told a C-Level executive that the company needed a Customer Loyalty program, they would often say "that's interesting, what do you mean? How would it work?" Today, if I make the same suggestion, I typically get a different response … "Do we really need one? Won't it be very expensive?" On the other hand, if I say to that same executive that they need a Customer Engagement Platform, ironically, they're likely to say "that's interesting, what do you mean? How would it work?"

Unfortunately, customer loyalty programs have come to be viewed by many C level executives as an expensive way to engage with one's customers. And CFO's are especially likely to view today's typical program as a needless expense. Recently, when meeting with the Operating Partner of a major Private Equity firm that has a number of retail chains in their portfolio, he interrupted the conversation to ask "does every retailer really need one of these programs?" While challenging the need for a loyalty program, he later agreed that managing customer relationships was a critical component of managing a successful retail venture.

More than simply a matter of terminology, today's loyalty program "architects" suffer from a lack of the formal educational foundation that other professions require. Loyalty program design has been largely a self-taught craft, with most loyalty architects simply cloning the design of their competitor's program, or worse yet, copying the design of their favorite program which typically is the one they find most rewarding.

Mike Case presents an excellent course in the fundamentals for successful loyalty program design. He presents the case for Listening to the Customer as the first step in developing a program that responds to the needs and interests of the customer. Using my favorite example, he illustrates how Brierley + Partners years ago heard Hertz customers tell us that they wanted a faster way to rent the car, not more points or golf balls. And interestingly, as we listened to the frequent renters' comments, we heard customers complain that even when I visit the same city each week, "no one knows my name", leading to the "name in lights" becoming a signature part of the Hertz #1 Club Gold.

Mike emphasizes the importance of identifying and embracing one's best customer, something that was fundamental in the early airline programs. Early in Brierley + Partners decades-long relationship with United Airlines, we noted that 25% of the revenue came from as few as 2% of United's customers, leading me to coin the "2-25 Rule." Early on, we found that cultivating a relationship with this 2% segment was critical to our clients' success.

And, as Mike explains, in loyalty design, the heart of the melon is identifying the "category heavy splitter," e.g. the weekly traveler who splits their travel between two of more airlines or hotel chains. If you can motivate these "splitters" to concentrate their patronage, you quietly gain share.

Mike joined Brierley at the dawn of what I call "Loyalty 2.0." With the widespread adoption of the internet and email, loyalty programs were able to dramatically reduce the cost of enrolling customers and communicating with them. Thus, with the costs for direct mail eliminated, programs were able to profitably invite a much larger segment of customers to participate.

One of Mike's first assignments at Brierley was leading the team that supported our Blockbuster account, then the dominant entertainment delivery brand. Designed after extensive research and months of careful in-market piloting, Blockbuster Rewards was one of the best examples of the use of "cadence" and "thresholds" to profitably drive desired consumer behavior. Mike tells how the Blockbuster Rewards program drove incremental revenue both at accrual as customers rented more to earn rewards and at redemption as they returned to the store sooner to claim free rentals. As Loyalty 2.0 evolved, retailers started to measure success less by stealing share from competitors and more by measurably stimulating an extra store visit.

It's exciting to see Mike share his career experience across a number of major brands. For anyone engaged in managing customer relationships, Mike's book is a must read. And, for consumers curious about the inner workings of the programs they enjoy, the book is a quick read while you're chasing your next upgrade. While there are many nuances to profitably driving the desired customer behavior, the basics are here for the taking.

Most importantly, in today's world where many marketers feel they are a qualified loyalty program architect, if you are indeed a self-taught architect managing a program, I trust the lessons in the book will be obvious tenets for continuing your success.

- Hal Brierley
Founding CEO, Brierley + Partners;
CEO The Brierley Group;
Entrepreneur in Residence at the Brierley Institute for Customer Engagement SMU Cox School of Business

Dedicated to the many team mates who contributed to so much success, including:

John, Veronica, Jennifer, Donna, Diana, Cory, Pat, Shawna, Mike, Jack, Tim, Sarah, Rob, Margie, Ed, Ginger, Laura, Whitney, Natalie, Michael, and Kam.

"There's these things called books, it's like television for smart people."

- Robert Redford as Bill Bryson in *'A Walk in the Woods'*

TODAY'S LOYALTY MARKETING: CONCEPTION

Fortunate early steps set a successful journey

I joined American Airlines after business school, starting in Corporate Finance. My journey in loyalty marketing began a few years later when I accepted a position in American's Marketing Planning group. This group used customer-specific data to develop and execute one-to-one marketing strategies designed to influence travelers. American Airlines had become a pioneer in the field of structured customer loyalty programs in 1981, when they launched what is often credited as the first effective frequent flyer program: *AAdvantage*. To this day, the program remains American Airlines' most important marketing tool.

In 1998, I joined Brierley + Partners, an agency focused on designing and managing customer loyalty programs. Hal Brierley had founded Brierley in 1985 after serving as the one outside adviser for the launch of the AAdvantage program and launching Pan Am's WorldPass program while serving as Pan Am's VP of Sales and Advertising. Over the next seven years, I had the opportunity to work with the Brierley team on some of the most successful loyalty programs ever launched

Over the years, my journey with customer retention and loyalty marketing evolved. We were moving past the original vision of the early customer loyalty programs and had arrived at a new benchmark for a customer's commitment to a brand, one I now refer to as *Customer Devotion*.

An important part of any journey - understanding how others succeeded

My team members understand my commitment to their professional growth. My commitment to the team has always been that, when our professional relationships are over, I want them to feel that they have advanced professionally in their careers. Toward that goal, I spend time sharing success stories from other brands to augment the learning process. Many of these former colleagues have gone on to senior leadership positions and are doing innovative work. With the same goal for those who read this book, I'll use a similar approach.

A step change for an industry

In 2007, I was fortunate enough to join the founding leadership team of a start-up airline based in San Francisco: *Virgin America*. It would be months before we were actually flying, but the nearly impossible-to-clear hurdle of obtaining United States government approvals to operate an airline had been navigated. While a part of Richard Branson's global Virgin brand, United State law required that US airlines be majority-owned by US interests. Richard Branson had a minority ownership interest in Virgin America for the use of the brand name and his services promoting the airline. So, despite its big brand heritage, Virgin America was a standalone, start-up company with limited resources. While exciting, the challenges we faced preparing to compete in the US airline industry were tremendous. This American industry may be the toughest in which to achieve long-term profitability.

The US airline industry was deregulated in 1978, removing government-controlled fares and allowing for open competition among air carriers. During the first 35 years of deregulation, the industry is reported to have lost $60 billion on US operations. Beginning in 2012, what would become a long run of low oil prices coupled with an improving economy began to provide strong profits. But recouping the substantial long-term losses remain a significant challenge for the industry. Demonstrating long-term, sustained profitability is something the industry has yet to do. Despite these historical economic realities, the travel industry attracts considerable interest – and many failed start-up airlines.

Among the many interesting things about working for Virgin America was the company culture. By design, the original founders set about intentionally doing things differently from any other US airline – and differently from most other traditional business environments at the time. If you were fortunate enough to have flown Virgin America before they were purchased by Alaska Airlines, you have experienced this first-hand with the product.

MIKE CASE

The role I accepted at Virgin had a traditional airline title, which included something that referenced being the development leader for 'Loyalty Marketing'-- a standard title for senior Customer Relationship Management (CRM) roles across many industries.

During my third week with the company I was approached by a teammate offering to have my business cards produced -- one of the early steps at jobs that make new team members 'official'. When it came time to put my title on the card for a new airline that was charged with redesigning the flying experience, it just did not seem to make sense to use a traditional Marketing Leadership title.

So, I asked one of the senior founding leaders if I could simply 'make up' my position title. He glanced up from his desk; apparently no one had broached this idea yet. Virgin being Virgin, even as a tiny airline start-up, he pondered this for all of three seconds, nodded, and said, "Sure." Then we both went back to work. We were, after all, busy with the near-impossible task of launching a start-up airline with limited support and resources.

Airlines had historically referred to their customers as 'passengers'. Virgin had bucked this trend early on and we were referring to our future customers as 'guests'. With this backdrop, my business cards would reflect the responsibility of the new role: **Guest Devotion**.

This seemingly small detail had real impact.

As the big banks and other travel partners approached Virgin America with everything from launching a co-brand credit card to participating as partners in our yet-to-be-launched loyalty program, they all noticed the unique title. It sent a powerful message about the relationships we were going to form with our customers.

Even more importantly, the message did not seem lost on teammates both in the corporate office and those who would be working with guests at airports across the country. Despite being a start-up company in one of the most difficult start-up industries in America, we were all working toward one goal. We wanted our guests to love Virgin America. We were not striving for customer satisfaction or customer loyalty.

Our sights were firmly set on one thing - **_Guest Devotion_**.

The genesis of effective loyalty marketing

Consumers continue to experience changing technology that enhances the services they receive and provides companies additional information about their customers. The fundamentals behind these initiatives remain rooted in what successful brands have done during prior decades to achieve success.

American Airlines changes loyalty marketing

In 1981 American Airlines launched the AAdvantage program and immediately got the attention of frequent travelers across their flying network. While airlines had introduced customer programs before this, the AAdvantage program is credited as the first loyalty program in travel to impact customers in a material and measured way. The program shifted purchase preferences among members and had instant success in what was considered a commodity at the time – air travel.

The obvious question is why would American Airlines launch a customer program that would eventually change the way companies in almost every industry now try to manage their customers?

The answer to that question may not be so obvious. Sure, American was competing furiously with United Airlines and Delta Airlines and wanted to capture these competitive airlines' customers at every opportunity. But the AAdvantage program's initial goal was to address another specific issue. Until the early 1990s, the major airlines sold only a small percentage of their tickets directly to passengers. Most tickets were sold by travel agents who received lucrative commissions – in some cases up to 30% or more of the ticket cost.

The airlines cultivated travel agency relationships in order to influence the airline selections that agents made for their clients. However, having travel agents selling the majority of tickets created a problem for the airlines at the time.

It's hard to imagine now, but, for years, you could go to the airport, board a flight, and be asked for little identification. Passengers typically picked their tickets up directly from travel agents. In most cases, passengers could proceed directly to departure gates, where they checked in with gate agents who verified the name on the ticket with their records and could board flights.

During this time, travel agents provided airlines with the travelers name but minimal additional information. The agencies did not share additional customer information because they did not want the airlines to go around them and avoid paying agent commissions by selling directly to their customers.

What motivated airlines to want to know their customers?

With limited information on passengers, the airlines could not accurately track the travel patterns of individual customers. For example, it was difficult for American Airlines to know that a passenger who had been flying twice a month for over a year from their hub in Dallas to Chicago might have suddenly stopped flying with them. Or, similarly, which of their customers might have decreased their frequency on this route from twice a month to once every other month.

Knowing Customer transaction information is key to success

Having the ability to track customer transactions to unique individuals opens a wealth of marketing power. Companies can monitor changes in buying habits. Is the company getting an increasing number of purchases, a decreasing number, or consistently similar purchases? Effective companies use this information to create strategies which build relationships with customers and then manage these unique customer relationships.

American Airlines surmised that if they could track their customers, they would know when customers appeared to be decreasing usage – "defecting" to another provider. Or when a customer appeared to be growing in share. With this knowledge, they could communicate appropriate promotional offers depending on their goals with a particular customer. The goal of effective CRM is not to over-reward a loyal customer. However, there is considerable pressure to build brand preference, since you cannot afford to lose a high-value customer to a competitor.

So a key for the AAdvantage program design was that it gave passengers a reason to enroll - to provide their name, physical address, and contact information, and to identify themselves each time they traveled with American by providing their AAdvantage member number.

Seems simple right? Set up a database to track the travel of passengers, then award credit for that travel that ultimately could be used for a free flight. American is reported to have spent over a year methodically engineering the AAdvantage program and building the technology to track and manage the program.

With all that, what could go wrong? Well if measured against their initial goals and plan – the answer is *everything*.

The Best Laid Plans...

American Airlines launched the AAdvantage program on May 1, 1981. The reaction among frequent travelers was both explosive and immediate, with thousands of travelers signing up for the program. United Airlines was one of American's most direct competitors at the time and seemingly had no idea that American was going to launch this type of program.

Almost immediately after AAdvantage was launched, the United Airlines team launched their own program, *Mileage Plus*. While American had spent considerable time engineering every aspect of their program and built technology for tracking and redeeming the program currency (miles), United Airlines sped to market with a competitive program that did not allow this luxury. It did not appear United had closely examined the initial AAdvantage program's terms and conditions.

In order to provide a proof of concept, AAdvantage was initially launched as a one-year promotion. Travelers could earn miles over a 12-month period and use those miles for free flight rewards if they achieved pre-set levels. The program was targeting frequent flyers, with a goal of capturing the top 10% of travelers who contributed over 50% of travel revenue at the time. American's goal was to carefully monitor and measure results and then either end the program or extend it for another year (or indefinitely) as the economics justified.

United launched Mileage Plus with few restrictions. The earning and redemption terms were open-ended. In theory, the program went on in perpetuity and miles never expired, meaning you could earn miles over many years to eventually use for free flights. This structure meant even the most infrequent flyers and those least loyal to an airline could eventually earn a free flight.

Under the pressure of United's seemingly knee-jerk response, American was forced to match United's much less stringent terms, which meant removing restrictions on the timeframe to earn or redeem miles. This put tremendous pressure on the economics of the airline programs during the 1980s as airlines were forced to accrue tremendous liabilities on their books for the miles accumulated by program members. After every major US carrier launched 'me too' frequent flyer programs with the same design, many economists questioned whether the programs made sense for the industry.

The Airlines save their Programs

During the late 80s, the airlines landed on an idea which would drive billions in revenue. They began selling miles, at a huge margin, to partners who used the miles to encourage airline program members to stay at partner hotels, rent partner cars, acquire partner credit cards, and even choose partner telecom providers. This 'side-business' turned into a multi-billion-dollar business for the large carriers and is widely credited with saving the programs during the early years until they could evolve back to more economically-friendly earning and redemption terms. The business of selling loyalty program miles is typically set up as a separate business unit at major airlines. During economic downturns, when large airlines struggle – even to the point of bankruptcy, these business units become the only profitable part of the organizations.

Many travelers now earn more of their miles on the ground than by flying. This is particularly true for program members who use the airline programs' co-brand credit cards.

Pioneering a new Marketing Science

Within ten years, every major US airline launched programs with essentially the same earning and redemption structures. Within fifteen years, every major flag carrier around the world adopted fundamentally the same program structure.

During the same period, industries from nearly all consumer categories began trying to create similar customer relationships by launching customer-facing programs.

Why is customer loyalty important?

Most, perhaps all, companies focus on attracting new customers to their business. For already successful companies this is a prime marketing focus. For a newly-launched brand, it is often the sole marketing focus. But if founders were to assume, even for a start-up company, that there would eventually be some level of success, they must begin to expand their marketing goals. Once you start acquiring customers, you must start thinking about how to retain them or maximize their long-term revenue -- typically referred to as a customer's *lifetime value*.

As companies begin to have success with new customer acquisition, they typically realize something important about their business:

Even a small percentage of customer attrition against a growing and sizable customer base becomes a substantial amount of lost revenue.

It costs less to keep a customer than acquire a new one

You have probably heard that expression a time or two, or fifty-two...

But despite this being true, a surprising number of companies across many industries put somewhere between marginal and zero effort into retaining their highest-value customers. Or companies go down misguided, ineffective CRM paths.

With the wildly growing popularity of Loyalty Marketing, many individuals now claim to be customer loyalty specialists.

What you will find, or have already found, is that most 'customer marketing' or 'relationship' efforts center on sending current customers offers – often untargeted -- to get them to buy more of a company's goods or services. This alone is not effective customer retention and over time can even drive customers away from the brand.

However, to be clear, when you are developing strategies to retain customers, to develop total customer devotion, you are specifically designing ways to keep them interacting with the company and, yes, buying more. The difference is that it should not feel to the customer that they are being solicited with irrelevant communications in order to encourage them to make additional purchases.

Relationship

Brierley + Partners trademarked 'Relationship Management' in the mid-1990s, long before others found the need to add the word 'Customer'.

A key to successfully increasing customer retention is the mindset that both corporate and customer-facing employees should have regarding structured customer programs.

The program is not a loyalty program.

It is not a frequency program.

*It is a **relationship** program.*

Additionally, as I will share, customer relationship marketing may not even be perceived as a 'program' by customers. Well-designed customer relationship marketing strategies serve as a tool which, when used effectively, allows a business to build deep, individualized relationships with customers. I'll plant that seed here and revisit often.

The Key to the Customer Devotion Opportunity

The challenge that most offline, online, or multi-channel transactional brands face can be summed up in one word: ***Splitting***.

The reason companies across most industries embark on customer loyalty programs is that without well-structured marketing and incentives most customers will 'split' their purchases between multiple providers. American Airlines understood during the seventies that many of their customers were flying competitors, such as United and Delta Airlines, to destinations that American also served. Key reasons for splitting included price, a schedule that was more convenient for a trip, or an incident with American which may have created dissatisfaction. There was nothing of value lost when switching to another airline for travel at the time – no material reason to consolidate purchases with one travel provider.

During years of both consulting and working directly for competitive brands I have consistently found across top consumer brands in such diverse categories as retail, travel, financial services, and entertainment that even customers who like and value a particular brand will often buy half or more of the goods and services they could have purchased from the brand through competitors. For example, a woman may be a regular shopper and value the clothing sold by *Ann Taylor* or *Forever 21*. But research will typically show that even most women who highly rank a particular brand are purchasing 50% or more of the clothing they could have purchased from these brands at competitors.

This isn't limited to women's clothing brands; it is true for most competitive brands – or certainly for companies who have not created effective Customer Loyalty initiatives or unique incentives to encourage consolidation of a consumer's purchases with the preferred brand.

Understanding Splitting

For some brands, competition for their customer's revenue may not be immediately obvious. Consider a company such as *Office Depot*. They sell electronics, office furniture, office supplies, and other home office products. The highest-margin items for a retailer in this category are the office supplies and furniture – as margins are often thin for computers and electronics. Not surprisingly, for the highest-margin categories there are several non-traditional competitors. Most grocery and drug stores carry a limited inventory of the most often purchased office supplies. Target, Walmart, and many others carry office supplies and often office furniture. What happens in this example – barring true *Customer Devotion* – is that even many 'loyal' Office Depot customers end up making convenience purchases of these items when they are in, or near, these competing brand locations or from many online options.

Splitting can even cross into competing products or activities. There are many examples of this with entertainment companies who compete for their customer's time with other entertainment options.

Theatre chains, for example, compete with other theatres, movies at home, video games, sporting events, and other entertainment options.

If even your 'good' customers are splitting as much as fifty percent or more of their purchases – a goal of shifting a small portion of this spending back to your brand can impact your bottom line. Typically, shifting as little as ten or fifteen percent of the purchases made with the competition back to your brand from a broad segment of engaged customers can result in TREMENDOUS revenue gains.

Why understanding splitting is so vital

Business leaders across many industries seeking to develop CRM initiatives frequently ask me this:

Can a Customer Loyalty Program create more demand from customers?

When the first airline programs were launched, they were specifically designed to reduce splitting. Travel providers operating these programs did not plan for their members to increase their overall paid travel. With a relatively high purchase price, travelers were not expected to purchase more flights. The primary goal for these loyalty programs was, and remains, to motivate travelers to pick the provider most often when they do travel, thereby shifting more of their travel to the brand. That was the goal for American to test when they launched AAdvantage and remains key for most customer loyalty initiatives today.

There are, however, consumer categories where well-engineered programs can and do result in incremental purchases. We'll come back to this important concept later.

There will be math involved, sorry...

For those of you who consider yourselves to be traditional 'Marketing' professionals, you may hate this. But today, more companies collect and have access to customer-level data than ever before. Being able to track activity at a unique individual customer level is vital. Effective analytics for developing, executing, and measuring marketing strategies make or break not just all loyalty marketing efforts, but ALL marketing efforts.

The leaking bucket

Years ago, a colleague shared a leaking bucket analogy to explain how successful brands grow customer revenue. I later illustrated that concept and have used variations of it both while consulting with clients and while working directly for revenue-challenged brands.

The analogy goes like this:

Imagine a water faucet pouring water into a bucket. The bucket has a number of small- to medium-size holes in the bottom, so at the same time water pours in, it is rapidly dripping out of the bucket from the holes. The bucket is half full, and in this example the bucket remains half full and does not fill up beyond the halfway mark.

The water flowing from the faucet is meant to illustrate the new customers transacting with the brand for the first time. New customers are largely a product of a company's customer acquisition efforts.

The water rapidly dripping out the bottom of the bucket is an illustration of customer defection to other brands. When the holes are too pronounced, and the leaking too great, the water leaks out of the bucket at the same rate that water is being poured in and the water level – which represents customer revenue – increases slowly or not at all. Or, worse still, the water leaks out faster than it pours in and the water level decreases. This represents brand revenue shrinking.

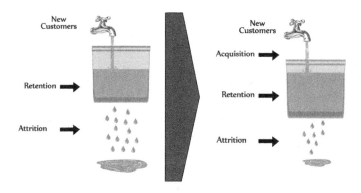

The illustration represents a similar number of customers leaking out and pouring in. The illustration also is a direct reflection of company revenue. Customers who have transacted with a company multiple times tend to transact more often, on average, than new customers. Therefore, losing even a small number of existing customers to competing brands can represent as much ongoing revenue loss in any given timeframe as the revenue gain from a much larger number of new customers.

The result, for publicly traded companies in this situation, is declining or greatly depressed stock prices. Private companies in this situation are typically soon seeking new senior leadership or a buyer for the declining asset. These outcomes result in unfortunate events for stockholders, private owner investors, and employees.

The goal becomes developing and implementing CRM efforts to reduce these 'leaks' which allow the bucket to fill – or in real world terms for brand revenue to grow.

LOYALTY STRATEGY DESIGN: ANALYTICS

Determining CRM opportunity and identifying success benchmarks

If customer level data exists, it is always the place to start to understand how to increase customer revenue. There are many aspects of customer behavior to explore toward these goals. But two key metrics define the state of the business and will serve as benchmarks for rolling out efforts to generate incremental customer revenue.

Analytics to support program design & implementation

Let's start with the customer database. Today, there are some clear advantages for developers of effective, actionable customer relationship management strategies. For several decades, companies across many industries have been working hard to collect and track customer data. The rise of the internet as a sales channel has also facilitated more effective customer level tracking.

This data will ultimately be used to track and measure customer behavior. But for initial loyalty strategy development, start by determining two benchmarks which measure the effectiveness of:

1. Building brand preference among <u>new</u> customers
2. Retaining <u>existing high-value</u> customers

Step 1: Loyalty marketing should begin with new customers

New customers will have the least loyalty to your brand. For transactional businesses such as retailers, travel providers, service providers, etc., the new customer is the one who transacts with you – most commonly in the form of a purchase – for the very first time. We'll address subscription businesses later, but the same fundamentals will apply.

On average, the most difficult segment of customers to get to purchase from you again are going to be new customers who have tried you once.

You can think of it this way: if this was a wager made in your office's coffee break area, how would you respond? "Assume we have a group of a thousand customers who made purchases recently and you have access to both their purchase history and demographic attributes. Now assume you can access only one customer attribute. What attribute would you want, and could you predict with high probability which customer segment is least likely to shop with you again?"

MIKE CASE

Yes, this can be done. The single attribute you would want is the total number of transactions the customer has made with your brand. The group of customers who have made only one purchase with your brand are the least likely to purchase again. Of course, there are ways to refine this answer.

Also, "first transaction with your brand" can be defined as a specific timeframe without purchases before this transaction. This may not mean since the beginning of time: it might mean within the prior 24 months, 36 months, etc. It's important to set a historic timeframe (typically 2-5 years) and use it consistently over time. My experience is to typically use 3 years, however this can be modified depending on the category of goods or services offered by the brand. Whether you use 12 or 36 months may not be that important. What is important is to establish a benchmark timeframe which you can then track over time.

For customers who have done business with you, the most difficult subsequent purchases to get follow this pattern:

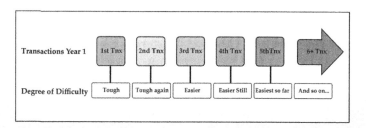

Among competitive brands, why is this almost always true?

With the first transaction a brand has now 'acquired' a new customer. The reasons more customers will drop out after one transaction than at any other frequency point are straightforward. The first purchase may have been a convenience purchase due to unique circumstances for a customer loyal to another provider. Or they may have just been trying out your product or service. Some of these new customers will become loyal, long-term, high-value customers. But a significant percentage will not do business with you again.

Retail and Travel are easy categories for illustration

Retail and travel provide easy examples, but this concept is the same for most industries.

Frequent travelers are a travel provider's most important customer. While working for La Quinta Inn & Suites, we had many new guest travelers stay at one of the properties because it was close to a destination they needed to be for a work assignment or a visit/vacation. If the guest travels frequently, this newly acquired customer has obviously been staying with competitors before this stay. There are many factors that determine if the guest will stay with LQ in the future, but for high-value travelers there is a good chance they have a preferred brand which will influence future decisions.

Consider a consumer who enjoys having many shoes to wear with different outfits or special occasions.

This customer has a last-minute event and makes a shoe purchase at a shoe store brand for the first time. Prior to this purchase, the customer has, of course, been buying shoes at competitors. In the ideal situation, the savvy new shoe brand collects information during the purchase that allows them to identify this new customer as someone who buys lots of shoes. Afterward, the shoe brand must target this customer and provide many reasons to buy shoes again from the brand.

While doing analysis on customer data across a range of industries, we found a consistent dynamic: the percentage of customers moving from the first to a second purchase is lower than from the second to the third and so on. Then, using total transactions with a brand as the variable, the next lowest percentage of customers making a subsequent purchase is going to be from the second to the third and so on as illustrated.

Why is this? Once a brand gets the second purchase, they begin to establish some purchasing habit from the customer who has now made an informed choice to buy from this provider again. And best yet, if you have established some type of customer loyalty initiative which offers benefits to customer for repeat purchases, they should now begin to have some type of growing equity for returning to your brand. Your focus is then on the third purchase, which statistically is typically 50% more likely than the second, and so on. For a standard transactional brand, attrition rates would typically look something like this:

CUSTOMER DEVOTION

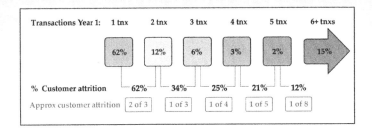

Any marketer working on retention should place a primary focus on getting the second transaction. This sounds so obvious, right?

Having worked on the corporate side with a range of companies and done consulting with dozens of others, I've found that few companies focus marketing in an impactful, targeted manner to achieve this obvious goal. As a first step determine the percentage of new customers making a second transaction. This becomes the benchmark from which to improve.

Step 2: Retain existing high-value customers

A key to success for this step is to understand who your best customers are.

If your company is already collecting customer-level data - and you finish this book and understand the principles - you have a tremendous head start. An important early analysis step I rarely see done in practice is to break the current customers into revenue deciles.

This relatively easy step yields tremendous customer understanding, which is vital for all levels of the organization. Additionally, it allows targeted marketing strategy development which can dramatically change the fortunes of your brand.

To accomplish this step, use the most recent twelve months of customer data. Unless there is a very significant and unusual economic event which occurred during the prior twelve months which is not likely to happen again, your most recent data is the best indicator of what customer behavior will be in the future. Put simply – barring a significant change - the future is most likely to be a repeat of the recent past. If there was a one-time aberration in the prior twelve months, use the most recent twelve months before the aberration.

Identify each unique new customer with transactions during the <u>first month</u> of your 12-month analysis timeframe and sum all transactions and revenue collected from these customers. A 'decile' is a term to define ten percent of the whole. Split customers into revenue deciles as equal 10% groups of customers based on the total revenue the customer spent with the brand.

The top 10% of customers based on revenue collected is Revenue Decile 1. Revenue Decile 2 is composed of customers from 10.01% - 20.00% based on revenue collected. Continue until revenue decile 10, which represents the lowest 10% (90.01-100%) of total customers based on total revenue spent by the customers during the 12-month timeframe.

With this analysis you are tracking new customers through their first-year lifecycle with the brand. Your goal is to work toward this data:

CUSTOMER DEVOTION

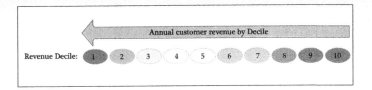

The 20% / 80% Rule

This is the often-cited Pareto principle. If you studied in a business program, this probably came up at some point. What has been shocking in my experience is how few companies do the analysis to understand customers and how this dynamic applies in terms of customer revenue.

The concept is that 20% of customers are often driving 80% of total brand revenue. If the principle holds – or something close to it - you can then focus finite resources and budgets toward highest-revenue customers and have an exponential impact on overall revenue.

I have found this rule to hold across the entire range of industries and brands I have worked with. While it may be 20% of customers = 70% of revenue, or 85% of revenue, the data will show high concentration of revenue among the best customers. While certain categories and brands may have unique characteristics, customer revenue will typically look something like this:

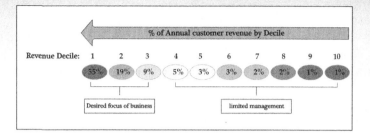

The little known 2% / 25% Rule

In managing customer relationships, there's an important subset of the Pareto principal that Hal Brierley has come to call the 2/25 rule. As part of understanding that some customers are much more important than others, for almost every category there is a core group of customers whose loyalty is very important to a company's profitability.

What you will often find is that as few as 2% of your customers can generate as much as 25% of your total brand revenue. It may be a little more or less, but it is almost always true that a very small percentage of customers account for a much higher percentage of total revenue. This dynamic holds true for airline and hotel brands and for luxury-good brands such as Neiman Marcus. With other categories you may find that the top 2% of customers account for a bit less revenue, but nonetheless you will find a high concentration of revenue.

Consider this: If a business has 10,000 customers, as few as 200 are generating as much as 25% of total revenue. It would seem you might want to know who those 200 customers are and treat them accordingly.

Big Data and what that implies

With the digital age, there is now more customer data available than ever before. Unfortunately, in many cases this seems to have translated into marketers being more lost than ever. The key to effective actionable customer insights is that all data is not created equal. We will therefore focus on the select data elements which are most critical to understand.

Since many companies are not accurately tracking relevant customer segments, what some of you may run into is what I refer to as 'hunch-based marketing'. Often, anecdotal, sweeping beliefs develop about how customers behave and what drives their decisions. Hunch-based marketing is common in corporate America.

What often happens is a small percentage of customers demonstrate certain behaviors that are undesirable for the brand. This small percentage of customers generates a disproportionate percentage of attention from the operations or customer service teams. From there, it is not uncommon that generalizations are made and often applied to a much larger customer group than actually exists. Additionally, there are times when policies or rules are developed and enforced to control these isolated circumstances which have an adverse effect on a broad group of valued customers.

Understanding the customer data = Advantage, you.

If you have accurate data and can direct effective analysis, you cannot ever be wrong. Reporting the behavior tracked in the data is always factual. However, you also may have heard that "numbers can tell any story someone wants them to."

This can be true as well, which is why it's imperative that you use the right approaches for analysis. Follow the customer-level analysis principles we've covered, and will cover, and you can credibly demonstrate what is happening to customers. This is why, with a well-built analysis strategy against credible customer data, you simply cannot be wrong.

Customer-level transactional data is the most powerful data you will have. Period. End of story. There are many other metrics that can and should be tracked. But the starting place is transactional, including revenue. When working to achieve Customer Devotion, this data is something you should not only care about, but care about passionately.

The power of RFM

I have interviewed a number of data analytic candidates for manager positions within my teams over the years. They have come from both consulting and corporate-side companies. I often ask this question:

"What does RFM stand for?"

While this is a fundamental element for any credible customer segmentation, about half of the candidates coming from a customer-level analytics foundation are not able to answer the question. The answer provides one of the fundamentals of effective customer level analysis.

RFM is an acronym which identifies three important attributes about a customer's activity with a brand.

R = Recency. When was the customer's last transaction or interaction with your brand? Recency is tracked as number of days since a customer's last transaction with the brand.

F = Frequency. How often has this customer transacted with your brand? This measures total transactions. This can be since the beginning of your data, or defined as the last 12 months, 24 months, 36 months, etc.

M = Monetary. How much total revenue has the brand collected from this customer? Timeframes should coincide with the definition used for the frequency metric.

The predictive power of each attribute is most often in the order of the acronym. The weight on recency would typically be higher than frequency, and frequency more powerful than monetary.

These attributes allow segmentation of the customer's likelihood of purchasing from the brand again, as well as the customer's projected future lifetime value. Lifetime value = LTV.

In most goods and service categories with a relatively frequent purchase cycle, a low recency score indicates customers most likely to return. If the customer has made multiple purchases with the brand and has a high frequency score, this indicates higher value, and if the customer tends to spend a large amount with each transaction, they have a high monetary score, indicating high value.

A straightforward way to approach a segmentation is to create a customer distribution using each of these elements.

Recency – 1 to N days since last purchase

Frequency – 1 to N total purchases

Monetary - $1 to $N average revenue per purchase

Then break each segment into equal thirds based on the distribution. This creates a 3 X 3 X 3 matrix with 27 segments. This could be simplified by breaking the monetary element into 2 groups of top 50% and bottom 50%, reducing the segments to 18. If the desire is to reduce segments, then start with the least important variable, which can vary based on the business but is most typically monetary, and work backwards.

For this example, we will code each segment, starting with Recency, as follows:

- *RT* is the top most recent third of customers
- *RM* is the middle most recent third of customers
- *RB* is the bottom most recent third of customers

Use the same naming convention for frequency: FT, FM, and FB. For simplicity of illustration, we will segment the monetary variable into top half and bottom half, MT and MB. The segmentation becomes 3 X 3 X 2 = 18 segments, as follows:

CUSTOMER DEVOTION

Segment Number	Segment Code	Recency	Frequency	Monetary	Customer value
1	RTFTMT	RT	FT	MT	Highest
2	RTFTMB	RT	FT	MB	
3	RTFMMT	RT	FM	MT	
4	RTFMMB	RT	FM	MB	
5	RTFBMT	RT	FB	MT	
6	RTFBMB	RT	FB	MB	
7	RMFTMT	RM	FT	MT	
8	RMFTMB	RM	FT	MB	
9	RMFMMT	RM	FM	MT	
10	RMFMMB	RM	FM	MB	
11	RMFBMT	RM	FB	MT	
12	RMFBMB	RM	FB	MB	
13	RBFTMT	RB	FT	MT	
14	RBFTMB	RB	FT	MB	
15	RBFMMT	RB	FM	MT	
16	RBFMMB	RB	FM	MB	
17	RBFBMT	RB	FB	MT	
18	RBFBMB	RB	FB	MB	Lowest

Once you understand this concept and can perform or direct manipulation of data to answer questions using RFM, you are well on your way. In the example we used equal thirds for recency and frequency and equal halves for monetary, but there is science and art in how to best leverage the data for effective segmentation. Both recency and frequency are powerful variables, and it may make sense to break them more finely and not into equal percentages. For example, the most recent 10% may be a segment, followed by the next most recent 40% then the final 50%.

Once you have implemented RFM, additional modeling can yield stronger targeting. Depending on the size of the customer base, there can be hundreds of cells used in both analysis and marketing execution. Few companies evolve this far, but my teams have achieved this working with many brands and it was a key component of our success.

MIKE CASE

The interesting thing about data models

Sophisticated data modeling is used to identify which variables are predictive of future behavior. These models are often difficult to explain to non-technical leaders or clients - even for the analytic resources who build them. They use statistical software to measure a range of customer attributes (e.g. how much a customer spends per transaction, what items the customer purchases, etc.) and determine which attributes are more prevalent among a group of customers doing one activity (like buying again and again) versus a group of customers doing another activity (such as not buying again).

Often, differences in data attributes between 'good' versus 'bad' customers are subtle and are only meaningful when several attributes interact in certain ways. So why does this matter?

It matters for the person responsible for developing and executing marketing strategies and campaigns to influence behavior.

A marketer whose sole goal is to build tremendous customer loyalty – true **Customer Devotion** - must develop messages, incentives, services, and other interventions at the individual customer level to create more of the desired behavior (typically, repeat purchases) among customers who are not exhibiting enough of the desired behavior.

If it is unclear why customers are no longer purchasing from the brand or are purchasing less often over time, then it is difficult to engineer marketing strategies, campaigns, and messaging to influence customer behavior.

Because of this, it is valuable to analyze independent variables in the customer data to determine how they influence future behavior.

For example, consider two hotel customers, Ed and Laura.

Both Ed and Laura begin staying at a hotel brand for the first time at the beginning of a given month. They both have a two-day stay each week during the month. They both spend about the same per night at the hotels. Traditional RFM modeling would say they both have an equal chance of coming back for a fifth stay. However, deeper analysis reveals this: Ed stayed at the same property each of the four times. Laura stayed in 4 different properties over the course of the month.

If we find a large sample of customers that look identical to Ed and Laura in terms of these attributes, we can then track those customers over time. What we then see is that customers staying at multiple properties are more likely to stay loyal over time. With this data as fact, we might hypothesize that the customer staying at the same location may have been on a temporary assignment and the hotel was convenient for their needs. But when the assignment ends, they may choose a different brand at the next location. The other guest appears to be consciously choosing the same brand each time at different locations and therefore may have more brand affinity.

In any event, the data shows different trends for each customer segment. Marketing should then test different communication approaches for these groups going forward. Discounts or bonuses for further stays may be necessary for the group of Eds, while the Lauras may receive appreciation and recognition along with reinforcement of the brand strengths to encourage future stays.

Beyond RFM

The previous example illustrates moving beyond traditional RFM to achieve more effective targeting. Testing independent variables in isolation – such as 'number of properties stayed' – allows you to determine what other independent variables are predictive.

This is accomplished by taking a random group of customers who all had transactions during the same timeframe in the past, isolating customers with each possible outcome of the variable, and tracking them over time. Identify if customers with a certain value for the variable have distinctly better, or worse, ongoing behavior. For example, a company selling streaming movies could isolate what type of movie the first purchase was and then track behavior to see if this variable is predictive of future customer value as follows:

New customers tracked for 12 months						
Purchase Category	Segment Type	Quantity	Total Transactions	Avg Transactions	Total Revenue	Avg Revenue
Romance	First purchase Jan Current year	#####				
Drama	First purchase Jan Current year	#####				
Comedy	First purchase Jan Current year	#####				
Action and Adventure	First purchase Jan Current year	#####				
Thriller	First purchase Jan Current year	#####				
Documentary	First purchase Jan Current year	#####				
		Total				

CUSTOMER DEVOTION

Data modeling identifies which variables are predictive and models their outcomes. This analysis goes beyond RFM and independent variable analysis. Modeling can provide significantly better results, moderately better, or limited improvement. The RFM variables are typically the strongest variables identified in the data model. Data models also seek to identify correlations between multiple variables which can be predictive – meaning that if two independent variables have specific values at the same time, they have a predictive nature.

While data modeling can increase the effectiveness of the segmentation, the exercise may not yield information as to the profile of the model's segments which is actionable in marketing. What this means is the model may optimize targeting based on the correlation between multiple variables but without insight into what causes customers to make decisions which create these correlations marketers may not be able to communicate effectively to motivate desired behaviors. For example, knowing that hotel guests staying on weekdays are likely business travelers can be leveraged in marketing communications. Or knowing that the customer has a high probability of owning pets, is a veteran, has grown children, etc. If there is predictive data that can be used to shape marketing communications, it becomes significantly more powerful when it shapes communications.

Consumer Research

Changing paradigms – the power of listening to your customers

Customer level data can allow you to know what customers are doing. What it does not always tell you is <u>why</u> they demonstrate the observed behaviors.

You also may find yourself in a situation where the company is not collecting individualized customer data. This of course lends itself to creating a structured program with incentives for customers to provide information at the point of sale to begin tracking customers. To support that effort, along with other marketing objectives, the best way to begin to understand why customers make the decisions they do is to ask them.

Qualitative versus Quantitative research

Qualitative Research

Qualitative research typically collects feedback from small groups of consumers. Focus groups, telephone interviews, or intercepts at stores are examples of qualitative research.

Qualitative is defined as a scientific method of observation to gather non-numeric data. What that means is that qualitative properties are observations done in a manner that does not provide statistical certainty of their accuracy. Qualitative research should focus on the identification of key values, needs, drives, emotions, and rational arguments for choices regarding a product or service and how providers are chosen.

Most commonly, qualitative research is conducted using focus groups. With an objective of getting feedback from customers about perceptions of brand, product, use of competitors, and other attributes, focus groups are typically conducted with 8-12 participants using a moderator with an outline of the areas of feedback to be collected. Many times, these sessions are conducted at facilities which allow sponsors to observe the sessions behind glass. Since they personally watch, many marketing professionals feel they are getting first-hand feedback and gravitate to this type of research.

Marketing professionals correctly love the idea of actual customer, or prospective customer, feedback and may view sitting behind a one-way mirror for a few hours as an easy way to accomplish this.

Understanding what factors influence customer decision-making, and influencing those factors, are key to success. Without feedback from customers, marketers can be left using 'best guess' as to what factors, benefits, or rewards may influence customer purchase decisions.

Quantitative Research

Quantitative research is defined as the systematic empirical investigation of feedback in a manner which provides statistically valid conclusions to be drawn from the data. Quantitative research is typically done using online surveys. Existing customers can be drawn from a company's database or from panels that exist using external service providers to identify customers and execute surveys. Prospective customers can be drawn from external panels as well. Using this approach, feedback can be gathered from thousands of respondents.

What is the best research approach for loyalty strategies?

The answer here is: do them both.

Without time or budget constraints I would do qualitative research first to get feedback and then test the hypothesis developed using quantitative research to get statistically accurate data.

If there are time and/or budget restraints which limit what research can be performed, my approach would always be to use quantitative research. The depth of feedback which can be obtained from thousands of respondents and having statistically valid data is invaluable. Respondent segmentation similar to what is done with customer data can also be performed. Done correctly, you can obtain powerful customer feedback.

While I'm a big believer in qualitative research, it is among the most misused tools in American business today. Since the techniques for best practice quantitative research with customer segmentation are analytical, some traditional marketers favor the easier process of sitting behind a one-way mirror and observing small groups of customers. However, challenges can arise with a small number of customers where a couple of participants may influence the overall discussion. Decisions are then made which may or may not be consistent with beliefs from a much larger customer set.

Research objectives

The table below outlines your primary research goals. While they would be similar for both qualitative and quantitative research, only quantitative provides statistically valid information.

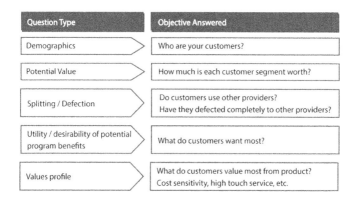

Question Type	Objective Answered
Demographics	Who are your customers?
Potential Value	How much is each customer segment worth?
Splitting / Defection	Do customers use other providers? Have they defected completely to other providers?
Utility / desirability of potential program benefits	What do customers want most?
Values profile	What do customers value most from product? Cost sensitivity, high touch service, etc.

The power of listening to customers

While listening to their customers, Amazon heard loud and clear that a tremendous pain point was the cost and time related to product shipping versus going down the street to a retailer. They removed this pain point by crafting Amazon Prime.

Having lived downtown in several metro areas through the years, I have a lot of experience using cab services and am well aware of the shortcomings of the industry. Customer feedback and new technology translated into a better model for consumers with Uber and LYFT– whose services I now use extensively.

Many of these new approaches come from a simple place – the product or service falls short of consumer expectations in some obvious (in hindsight) manner. Listening to customers: this phenomenon did not start with the rise of the digital age. While the methods of data collection have changed over time, the research science has been used for decades.

As illustration of the power of listening to customers I'll share an example. This case study is from long ago but has relevance for many of today's challenges.

Hertz Rent a Car changes the industry

After seeing the demonstrated success of the early airline loyalty programs, Hertz engaged Brierley + Partners to design a structured customer program. Given the airlines' success, Hertz specifically wanted to launch their own program allowing customers to accumulate points which could be used for rewards.

However, research with frequent travelers who rented cars revealed several key insights:

- By the late 1980s, frequent travelers were typically in airline programs and were already collecting

- miles and were not interested in earning another program's currency.
- Many of these travelers asked simple questions:
  - "You know I'm coming. How come I have to wait in the same long line Monday mornings when I arrive in the city where my project is every week?"
  - "I fly to Tulsa every week. How is it that no one on your team ever seems to know who I am?
- Based on insights collected from customers, the first-of-its-kind program, *Hertz #1 Gold*, launched in 1989.
  - Hertz became the first car rental company to allow program members to bypass lines, go directly to their pre-reserved cars, and exit parking lots with a simple checkout.
  - Hertz installed #1 Gold boards at each airport rental car lot, where members were recognized with their 'name in lights' indicating where to locate their cars.

The successful solution at that time was to design and implement an easier way to rent a car. The Hertz #1 Gold program solved major pain points for frequent renters. Customers saved time by bypassing lines and were recognized as valued customers with their name in lights.

While Hertz was convinced they needed a points program, the Brierley + Partners approach included listening to customers. It became clear what changes customers wanted and what impact it would have on their car rental preference. This approach was revolutionary at the time and gave Hertz an immediate competitive advantage. Since then, all major car rental companies have invested in similar infrastructure and processes.

LOYALTY STRATEGY DESIGN: COMPONENTS

Designing a customer loyalty program

Many professionals associate loyalty programs with earning points. While there can be tremendous benefits to using points as a currency to encourage select behaviors, there are additional benefits which should be considered when designing effective CRM strategy. Additionally, accumulating a reward currency is not always the best solution – consider Amazon Prime.

Categories of Loyalty Program Benefits

Loyalty program benefits generally fit into six categories and should be considered and combined based on customer analysis and the objectives for customer behavior. In some cases, benefits from all categories are offered to all program members, or benefits can be added for select program member segments. The most effective categories include:

Access

- First to have opportunity to buy new merchandise

By Invitation Only

- 'Invite only' special events

Recognition

- We recognize you as a best customer; we know you by name

Appreciation

- Thank you

When executed effectively, never underestimate the power of a simple 'thank you'.

Services

- Dedicated customer service with expedited access; free shipping; etc.

Rewards

- Free or discounted goods and services

The benefits within each category are virtually limitless depending on your product or service and capabilities. Traditional brick & mortar businesses can offer dedicated check-out lines, member-only parking spaces, and other benefits. Online businesses offer free expedited shipping upgrades, access to dedicated specialists who provide advice remotely, and many other benefits.

Many new program launches are dependent on structured rewards. But points and/or structured rewards are not always the answer. Let's examine a successful program launch which did not use structured rewards and remains a relevant example for many current brands.

Customer engagement where people expect it least

Many business professionals do not believe you can drive customer engagement or relationships in low-engagement categories such as utilities or infrequent transactional categories such as mattresses.

Local phone service across the United States was largely a monopoly from its inception through the 1990s. This was necessary during the initial build of phone infrastructure to encourage the few companies who ultimately controlled the service to make the enormous investments necessary to update and maintain the infrastructure. This created monopolies for a few companies who controlled the service for all consumers. Monopolies do not lend themselves to the best consumer experience, however, and during the 1990s the US government deregulated local phone service. This was accomplished by requiring the companies who had built the infrastructure to lease their lines, at a wholesale rate, to what would become competing companies.

MIKE CASE

While hundreds of companies got into the business of selling local phone service, only a handful had success. One of those successful companies was Sage Telecom. Sage began offering local phone service to homes in 1996. They grew rapidly and by 2004 had 550,000 customers in 13 states. But the landscape for local phone service was changing dramatically at this point as cable TV and internet service providers entered the market by also providing local phone service.

By late 2004, Sage began to lose more customers than they were acquiring and were shrinking as a company. The company founders realized that at some future point their service and company were going to rapidly lose value. While Sage was still quite profitable, the founders believed they had a valuable asset and were considering options, including selling the company, though they knew that the value of a growing company is significantly higher than a company that is consistently shrinking. During this time, Sage approached me to lead marketing and customer analytics and I joined in early 2005. The challenge was to reverse negative growth trends in order to support a more profitable sale for the business.

Since the company was shrinking little by little every week, the growth objective needed to be reached quickly as the hole got deeper every day. We had to work fast.

My question for you at this point is: what was my first step? I hope your first thought was customer analysis. As a subscription service, Sage had near-perfect customer data and I knew a wealth of information existed if the data was analyzed effectively.

The work quickly uncovered tremendous customer acquisition challenges, which we will cover later.

How did we get to the finish line?

First, we identified highly profitable customer segments which had higher than average customer attrition. We held internal focus groups with customer service agents to understand customers and their pain points. We then listened to our customers using quantitative research.

Using this information, we developed and launched **Sage Select**

The program was offered to specific customer segments who met the greatest potential for success: high-value and higher-than-average risk of attrition.

Since they were existing customers and we were simply enhancing their service, we did not have to ask them if they wanted to join anything. First, we ran tests with statistically-valid small groups of customers to measure results, then expanded as we rolled out the program.

Sage Select customer communications and benefits:

- Customers who were upgraded to Select received a high print-quality mailing, reminiscent of a wedding or graduation announcement, that welcomed them to *Select* and shared the customer's new benefits.
- The Select customer phone bill was redesigned to have a recognition tone, utilizing colors such as gold to invoke a more upscale perception. The

monthly bill was used to reinforce the new Select Customer benefits.
- A special Select customer service number was established and shared on every Select communication or bill. Calls were routed to the top of the phone queue eliminating wait times on busy days.
- Select customers received free long distance on four *select* days throughout the year:
  - Thanksgiving
  - Mother's Day
  - Father's Day
  - Valentine's Day (which we positioned as 'Relationship day', a time when Select members could call – at no cost – anyone, anywhere, who was special in their lives).
- An Anniversary gift was sent to customers during the month they signed up for Sage service

When the announcement arrived communicating the new Select status, customers immediately knew something was different. No telecom company had sent them something of this quality, this personal, or showed they cared this much about their customers.

The phone bill was redesigned to feel different than both their former Sage bill and any utility bill they had ever received. The tone of messaging on the bill was recognition-based to convey who we were as a company – caring people trying to extend our best to our most valued customers.

The Select customer service line was answered by designated Select representatives who were chosen based on their experience and demonstrated care of customers. This proved an effective recognition tool internally, as representatives worked hard to qualify to become a Select service representative.

Free long-distance days were promoted as a way to help customers extend their personal relationships and thank them for the relationship they had with Sage Telecom.

The anniversary gift was sent during the month the customer initially signed up for our service, to celebrate their relationship with Sage. We sent Select customers an entertainment gift card which allowed them to see any movie at any theatre free or access free books or music.

We measured results using a random select test and control strategy. Without offering free service or structured rewards, the costs of execution were low. As we refined the customer targeting and marketing, the results were stunning. Select customer attrition was ultimately reduced by nearly 40%.

Improvements in retention along with refined customer acquisition strategies allowed us to reverse the significant negative growth trend and begin growing revenue within 10 months of my arrival.

With the changing landscape in telecom, Sage became the _only_ landline provider of scale in the country to grow their customer base during the next two years. At that point, the business was sold -- in a growth mode and at a significant premium.

Listening to customers revealed that a points program was not the answer. We needed to differentiate and, most importantly, *humanize* our relationship with customers. The path to grow the business, when no competitor was achieving similar results, was rocky – but there was tremendous pride for the team when we achieved our goals.

Designing Structured Rewards

The objective of customer rewards: create opportunity cost

Earning credit toward a future reward is often critical to influencing customer behavior. The airlines defined the model with their early programs: flyers accumulated miles they could later use for a free flight. Many companies now have similar approaches. Programs with structured rewards should be designed to create an "opportunity cost" for members if they choose to patronize a competitor, meaning that they will lose a benefit or reward that they value. .

Creating opportunity cost can be used with anything from the shampoo you buy to what movie theatre you choose. For this to work, rewards should have a perception of both appropriate and compelling value. If, for example, a pizza place offers you a free pizza after purchasing six pizzas, you may be compelled to always chose that provider versus being influenced to use the latest discount coupons you have received from competitors.

Rewards

There are many client service companies offering largely 'canned' loyalty solutions. Most commonly, client service companies build an automated points engine they sell as a plug-in process for a client's point-of-sale. If your analytics and program design steps lead you to a solution which involves using a program currency, it often makes sense to engage one of these companies.

You may have seen programs which allow customers to earn benefits based on purchasing goods or services over time. These might include:

- Spend $100 over time and receive $10 off a future purchase
- Spend $250 over time and receive a $40 gift card for a future purchase
- Buy 10 of a good/service and receive the 11th one free

The idea of a deferred savings or free reward can be achieved with points or simply by counting transactions. If the business has significantly different total purchase costs per transaction, then using points has advantages since the program currency earned can be linked directly to the revenue collected. If average transaction per customer is similar, then accumulating transactions can be a solution which is easily understood by consumers.

Let's consider fast food as an example. While it varies regionally, nationally most customers spend between $5.00 to $7.00, with an average ticket of about $6.00 per meal. Accumulating purchases may simplify a structured program for members - or at least purchases that include an 'entrée'.

Depending on the product or services being sold, how frequently they are purchased, along with other factors, determine which reward scheme will be most effective.

Structured rewards will be the most significant expense for any program which includes them. Poorly crafted reward structures can result in program economics which cannot be sustained, leading to a program's end. Careful consideration and testing should be used when designing rewards.

The power of the "Empty Seat"

What was it about the economics that worked so well for the airlines? Why have the airline programs remained so powerful?

For decades, the airlines blacked-out certain travel dates for free travel and only allowed a limited number of seats on each flight to be used for awards. These were the seats the airline did not expect to sell. So, while there may have been lost revenue from a free seat taken as a reward by a passenger who might have otherwise paid for it, a paying passenger was not 'displaced' or turned away because the flight was full.

The cost to the airline for this otherwise empty seat becomes the variable cost for passenger processing, amenities on board such as free drinks/snacks, and marginal fuel costs for the additional weight on the plane.

CUSTOMER DEVOTION

It's a very small real cost for the airline vs. the perceived value of the free ticket.

For decades airlines also offered award seats with a three-week advance purchase requirement. If seats were needed for travel sooner than three weeks out there were, of course, additional charges. Airline point-of-sale systems now typically embed the additional costs into the mileage requirements for the trip – e.g. increasing the miles required when booking close to departure.

When booking 2-3+ weeks in advance, ticket costs are generally substantially lower than when booking near travel dates, which is common for business travelers. So, while a roundtrip ticket between Chicago and San Diego bought 3 days before departure may be $1,800, a similar ticket bought weeks in advance may be only $400. Most program members take most or some trips for work reasons at the higher close to departure cost. Because of this airline program members tend to place a higher perceived value on their free ticket than the actual cost would be booking with the requirements of rewards seats.

The airlines, through careful planning or simple luck, landed on the perfect reward formula. High perceived value, low revenue dilution given a small chance of having otherwise sold the seat at full cost and low variable costs for putting a reward customer in the seat. **Bingo!**

As these programs have become common across industries, companies continue trying to figure out their own versions of the "empty seat".

The Most Effective Rewards

Your first objective for rewards

- A substantially higher perceived value of the award than its actual cost

When it comes to rewards, a company will always get stronger results if it can identify and use rewards with a higher perceived value than actual cost to the company. This contributed significantly to the success of the airline programs and was copied by other travel providers – e.g. the empty room for a hotel brand.

Crafting successful programs with many brands has allowed me to explore this objective across industries. Retailers who sell their own branded clothing as well as other designer brands typically have significantly different margins on their products. Macy's, for example, sells collared polo-style shirts with labels they have created and source themselves along with designer shirts from Polo, Izod, and other brands. In this example a 'free polo shirt' used as a reward would have a significantly lower cost if the shirt were Macy's own brand – even though the price of the shirt may not be significantly less than other designers. A shirt with a perceived value of $50 may have a cost of $12 for the in-house brand and $25 for designer brands.

The goal is typically to have at least twice the perceived value versus actual cost. More than twice is great, while less may be okay as well. For many companies, finding this sweet spot is not as easy as it may seem.

Currency earning and redemption cycles

A common question regarding program currencies involves point expiration. Should a member's points expire? The simple answer to that question is - yes.

Once rewards are determined, the next step is to design earning and redemption cycles which encourage incremental revenue behavior for members. Depending on the product/service purchase cycle, program design can set rewards to be redeemed or expire monthly, quarterly, annually, or over multiple years.

For example, while a consultant I led the strategy team which designed a program for American Eagle Outfitters (AEO) – a retailer targeting consumers in their teens to early 20s. Up to that time, every retail program in the United States had been launched with annual earning cycles or had no expiration.

What we found by listening to AEO customers was that, for a 17-year-old, being motivated by a reward a full year into the future felt like an eternity. By then, they would be in the next grade and just did not have a consideration process that far into the future (oh to be so young!) Additionally, as is common with clothing retailers, AEO brought in new merchandise each season – fall, winter, spring, and summer. A goal for clothing retailers is to encourage customers to shop during as many seasons annually as possible. Our analysis showed that a very small percentage of customers shopped during even three seasons and a very low single-digit percentage of customers shopped all four seasons.

So, we developed and worked with AEO to launch their new program, **AE All Access Pass**. The program allowed members to accumulate points based on purchases during each three-month season and then provided a reward in the form of a discount to use during the first six weeks of the next season. The discount ranged from 15% to 40% depending on the points earned. The redemption window was set to coincide with the introduction of new seasonal merchandise and expire before the late season discounts were applied to clear out unsold merchandise before the next season. The rewards therefore encouraged shopping during periods of full priced merchandise.

The program included other benefits, but the quarterly approach for the structured rewards was a first of its kind in clothing retail to encourage seasonal shopping and was engineered to be most effective for the target audience.

Reward program currency with expiration

You should either have some type of expiration policy regarding reward currency, or rules that require minimum activity levels for points to remain active. The reason is simple.

Suppose you really like soft-serve ice cream and Dairy Queen is your favorite place to buy it. However, on weekends you occasionally run errands in a part of town where there are no Dairy Queens and so, during these occasions, you stop at Sonic for your soft serve. Assume Sonic had some type of program that awarded you credits that never expire and you - being a savvy consumer - enrolled in the program. In this scenario, you would earn rewards for your purchases, eventually. The problem with this model is that even if it took you two years and you did not change anything about your behavior you could still earn the rewards. In this example Sonic does not get incremental revenue but incurs the cost of the rewards.

The goal of any type of incentive is to increase customer revenue. In this example, the member earns free goods – a cost to the sponsoring company – without any incremental revenue.

Neiman Marcus launched what is considered the first structured retail program, *Incircle*, in 1984. The program structure included a number of important elements (which is surprising, given they were one of the retail industry pioneers in the loyalty space).

The InCircle program, which included core design elements such as recognition and appreciation, as well as points which expired at a well-understood end-of-year interval, provided competitive advantage for a decade or more.

Participating in other company's loyalty programs?

The airlines generate tremendous revenue selling miles to partners which are used to influence airline program members to do business with those partners.

Early in my career at American Airlines, I worked in partner marketing selling AAdvantage miles to partners.

Years later, while working for a hotel brand, we purchased miles from several airlines. With our own loyalty program, customers could choose to earn miles or our points when staying. The strategy allowed us to acquire a limited number of new customers influenced by their airline's program. Despite this I would typically not recommend purchasing airline miles to influence your customers. Here's why:

- Cost. Miles are expensive. For the cost of a meaningful incentive using miles you typically can do something more impactful using your own goods/services.
- Limited Audience. No matter what business you are in, travelers who fly the sponsoring airline will be a limited subset of your customers – even if you are in a major airline's hub market. Your goal is to offer benefits that have appeal to the vast majority of your high-value-potential customers.
- Not tied to your brand. Allowing your customers to earn currency in an external loyalty program further vests those customers into the external loyalty program and sponsor – not YOUR brand. If the customer has a negative experience with your brand, they can switch to a competitor and not lose anything of value with your brand.

You want your customers loyal to your brand. When La Quinta Inn & Suites acquired a new customer, we always saw higher lifetime values from those earning Returns points vs. airline miles.

If it does makes sense to buy miles to attract new customers, a subsequent strategy to motivate these new customers to earn your own currency or benefits can be very effective. If you have a structured program with currency, you will probably find you can offer double or even triple credits for the cost of the miles. Targeting these offers selectively is motivational -- both to get a second transaction from a new customer and to move the customer acquired using miles to your program currency.

Multi-tender payment options

Many brands in retail, travel, entertainment, and beyond offer co-brand credit cards issued by partner banks. These cards usually allow consumers to purchase from the issuing co-brand partner with, at least initially, favorable interest rates, discounts, free shipping, and other benefits. In recent years many of the partner banks have evolved these cards to be bankcard association Visa or MasterCard, so they can be used with all merchants, not just with the co-brand partner.

These cards can be very profitable for the issuing financial institutions. And revenue sharing from these products -- from the issuing banks back to partners -- can result in a lucrative revenue stream. In general, these can be great products for both the financial institution and sponsoring partners.

However, despite what the financial partners offering your customers the co-brand card may tell you, when it comes to customer loyalty programs do not be confused. The co-brand card products alone should not be the foundation of an effective loyalty strategy. This is why:

even for an engaging retail brand, typically fewer than 20% of customers will apply for and receive the brand's co-brand credit card – and this percentage is often in single digits. With an end game of true Customer Devotion, you need to engage a higher percentage of customers. Additionally, you want to engage the 'right' customers – those who make significant purchases in your product category. Many of the customers who apply for partner cards are single-purchase customers seeking to take advantage of the offer to take the card. Some of you may have done this yourselves.

Why do you care about customers who prefer competitors? Because you want to convert them to YOUR brand. And there is no more cost-efficient and effective way than obtaining their name, address, email, and other information to establish a direct relationship with relevant communications, promotions, product offerings, and more.

Bank partners may feel their card product is threatened by a multi-tender loyalty initiative and I have heard proposals from banks that make loyalty programs contingent on using the co-brand card. But the truth for the bank partner companies is this: to build widespread, enduring customer loyalty you must allow your customers to purchase using the payment method of their choice. Attempting to change their behavior to purchase more often, as well as influence them to change the way they are most comfortable making their purchase, is a doubly difficult proposition – and one that will have limited success at best.

Your goal is to maximize your opportunity for success; in this case, it means letting customers pay using whatever means they prefer.

Can program benefits be engineered to stimulate incremental purchases?

As discussed, most loyalty programs should be justified using the premise that customers will not purchase more of the goods and services after becoming a member. Incremental revenue is generated by loyalty program members shifting purchases from other providers – reducing splitting.

However, there are examples where program benefits are engineered in a way to encourage incremental purchases. One of the best examples is from what used to be a powerhouse brand, but which now has only one retail location: Blockbuster Video.

In fact, Blockbuster Video is such a good example that it is featured at The Brierley Institute for Customer Engagement at Southern Methodist University Cox School of Business, the only academic institution offering a concentration in loyalty for MBA candidates majoring in Marketing. The Blockbuster program shows how having the right cadence and appropriate thresholds for earning credits and redeeming rewards can both minimize costs and drive incremental revenue. It also provides a vivid example that having a great loyalty program is not enough to save a great marketing brand which does not evolve when confronted with a changing competitive landscape.

Blockbuster Video

Some of you may not remember home movie rental giant Blockbuster. Competition from companies such as Red Box, Netflix, and, ultimately, on-demand movie options led to the demise of a brand which not only dominated movie rentals for the home but was also an entertainment powerhouse sponsoring a nationally televised and respected movie awards show.

While they did not react to the threat of Netflix and others, prior to these challenges Blockbuster did launch and operate a customer loyalty program that allowed them to overcome competitors on multiple retail fronts, reverse declining share, and dramatically increase frequency of rentals.

By the mid-1990s, many retailers had entered the movie rental market. This included most grocery stores, big box stores such as Walmart and Target, and even convenience stores such as 7-Eleven. An aggressive movie rental competitor at the time, *Hollywood Video* was also expanding, and for the first time Blockbuster experienced declining share of overall US movie rentals.

In 1997, Blockbuster retained Brierley + Partners to design a loyalty program. After a lot of listening to Blockbuster's customers, *Blockbuster Rewards* was launched in 1998. After joining Brierley, I led the team responsible for the launch and ongoing management of the program across North America.

Unlike other retailers at the time who could not easily collect individualized customer data, Blockbuster had a different model. To rent movies, customers had to sign up, provide their personal data, and then use a membership card with each transaction. This gave Blockbuster near-perfect customer data. The design of Blockbuster Rewards was especially genius at the time for several reasons.

It is much easier to get the Finance group to endorse a loyalty program which collects fees that fund much of the program cost. However, collecting a fee to join a program is a significant hurdle for many customers and can significantly reduce program membership. For traditional retailers who have an objective of collecting additional customer data, a program fee which will reduce enrollment is typically not appropriate. Blockbuster had near-perfect customer data because of their sales model. We launched a program that had an annual fee of $9.95. The top 2% of customers were enrolled as fee-waived Gold members and sent personalized program materials.

The program was tested in two waves in select cities. The activity of customers joining the program was measured to determine the optimal customer segments for the program based on incremental revenue generated by program membership. Once it became apparent which customer segments were most profitable, we worked with Blockbuster to offer the program to select customers who fit these profiles but were not joining the Rewards program, with a targeted first-year fee-waiver offer.

Blockbuster's average customer at the time rented fewer than four movies a month. The stores' videos were broken into two categories: "New Release" videos, located along the outer walls, and "Favorites" -- older movies which were displayed on shelves throughout the inside of stores. One challenge Blockbuster had at the time was that many customers just walked the outer wall looking for their rentals. They needed something to encourage customers to browse the Favorites inventory, which was much more profitable to Blockbuster.

Members received three primary benefits:

1. Rent 5 movies during a calendar month and receive a free rental -- New Release or Favorite --during the next calendar month
2. Rent a movie Monday through Wednesday and receive a free second Favorites movie rental
3. One free Favorite rental each month without restrictions

Seems simple enough, right? But powerful analytics supported those benefits.

1. Average customers rented fewer than 4 movies a month. These customers needed to rent more often to earn their free rental.
2. The free favorite Monday-thru-Wednesday encouraged customers to rent more often during slower weekdays. Customers who did rent on these days rarely rented two movies since most of them needed to get up early the following day for work or school. So, this benefit encouraged additional rentals with little lost revenue from the second rental.
3. Encouraged customers to explore the Favorites within the stores

Testing the program in select cities verified what our research and analytics had predicted.

- Stores had significant program enrollment rates, ultimately generating millions in fee revenue
- Customers who became members increased movie rental rates, typically renting more often on weekdays to take advantage of program benefits
- Rentals of Favorites increased significantly, including paid rentals

Blockbuster reversed the prior-year trend of declining movie rental share as their customers reduced splitting of movie rentals to other outlets in order to maximize their program benefits at Blockbuster. Additionally, the average number of rentals for members increased as they rented more often to maximize benefits. Benefits stimulated additional paid demand.

Despite the tremendous success of Blockbuster Rewards, a few years later Blockbuster's management did not react to the growing threat of competitors such as Netflix and Redbox who ultimately caused the company to fail.

Recognition tiers

Most structured programs are either launched with or evolve to have tier(s) for the highest revenue members. Often a program's top tiers are named after precious metals such as Gold, Platinum, etc.

I have been part of many discussions with senior management about whether to develop the higher-value tiers, since they typically have exclusionary benefits. Some companies feel they do not want to appear exclusionary to groups of their customers and may make an argument against program tiers.

Having done considerable testing with top tiers, I can say definitively that well-engineered top tiers drive incremental revenue. Recognition can be a strong motivator, and top-tiers should be designed to enhance recognition benefits for highest-revenue customers.

Top tiers must have additional or enhanced member benefits. Most commonly they involve enhanced customer service and recognition elements.

The 20% - 80% principle predicts that a small percentage of your customers would be in top tiers but would represent a disproportionately high percentage of total brand revenue. Offering additional service-oriented benefits to a small number of highest-value customers can often be accomplished without adding significant costs to the program.

Since members of these tiers are your highest-revenue customers, you have lots of motivation to help ensure they have a good experience.

Should you have top membership tiers in place when launching a new program?

If your business accurately tracks individualized customer data before the program is launched, then you can include a higher member tier at program launch. However, if one of the goals of the program is to begin collecting customer level data to accurately track customers, the program should be launched without tiers. Tiers can be offered later as 'upgrades' for select segments of most-valuable members once the data collected provides qualification criteria.

Publishing the criteria for top membership tiers can motivate members who qualify for the tiers to remain loyal to retain their status and motivate other members to increase their usage with the brand to qualify for top-tier status.

The airlines do this by publishing the miles, flight segments, or revenue that members must spend annually to obtain top-tier status.

The criteria should ultimately be linked to revenue but are more effective if communicated in a way that encourages the activity you want from customers. For example, a hotel brand that wants guests to stay with them more often would use a qualification level based on nights stayed, i.e. requiring 20+ nights to achieve Gold status. Or a theatre chain attempting to motivate customers could use a criterion of seeing 25 or more movies annually with the brand.

When Blockbuster Rewards was launched, customers were offered Blockbuster Gold Rewards if they had rented 100 or more movies or games in the prior twelve months. At the time, about 2% of customers rented at this level. A year after launching the program and communicating the criteria for reaching Gold status, the percentage of customers who rented 100+ movies annually doubled to 4%. This is the dynamic you hope to – or dream of – achieving with customers.

PROGRAM IMPLEMENTATION

There is a point when the analysis of customer data, research, and brainstorming benefits turns into a customer-facing marketing effort. When planning implementation, it is critical to define and set up measurement criteria as part of the plan. Despite the many success stories I will cite in this book, successfully impacting a broad segment of customers to have a material impact on your business is tough – very tough.

Barring a competitive reason to move forward with a company-wide rollout immediately, your approach should be to launch a controlled test, refine the marketing based on results, and then roll out company-wide.

Metrics to measure success

How do you measure Loyalty?

I love this question. It gets asked and debated constantly and is the topic of multiple books. Is the right measurement:

- Customer Satisfaction?
- Net Promoter Score?

- Social media interactions?

These are all good barometers and are often tracked by marketing teams. But none of them is the one true measure of success.

But there is one perfect barometer for customer loyalty, one that is inarguable, yet not often relied on with tenacious science to measure the results of CRM strategies. And this one 'truth' is the most difficult to impact significantly. The metric is: **customer revenue**.

When it comes time for the Chief Financial Officer to bless additional spending on customer retention marketing this metric will be the key. If accurately measured and justified, your CFO, President, and even the board of directors will quickly fall in line.

How to measure marketing results

Regardless of the diligence in the analytic stages of development, significant new customer marketing efforts should be tested first. Rolling out flawed marketing strategies broadly can have catastrophic results. Well-managed tests designed to gather statistically valid data dramatically limit the economic risks and help ensure longer-term success.

When planning a structured program, set it up initially as a 6- or 12-month test. This can be built into the terms of the program and not, at first, overtly communicated . This allows for either the discontinuation of the program if the test does not generate positive results or a plan to alter the approach to achieve positive results.

Testing when individualized customer data is available

If you are in a situation where you are tracking all customer transaction data, the testing approach is straightforward.

When testing any marketing efforts your goal is to structure the test in a manner which allows you to measure the revenue activity of customers exposed to the new marketing versus 'like' customers who are not exposed to the marketing.

All customers will not respond to marketing in the same way. Therefore, you should structure tests to include a broad range of customer segments. The segments will often be defined using RFM metrics, but often will include additional attributes depending on the business and consistent with the earlier segmentation topic covered.

Let's look at an example of the best approach:

Let's assume a customer loyalty program has been developed. Let's also assume we want to test two versions of the program. One has more generous reward levels which represent higher costs -- Loyalty Rich. The second has less generous reward levels -- Loyalty Moderate.

You will want to test these efforts against a range of customers.

CUSTOMER DEVOTION

Identify a statistically valid sample size for measurement. The higher the activity level of customers based on RFM metrics the smaller the sample size can be while providing accurate measurement. You may need to rely on analytic resources, or you can find formulas readily online.

For this example, we'll test with three categories of customer type: highly engaged customers, moderately engaged, and low engagement. We then random sample out 150,000 of each customer type as follows:

- Highly Engaged Customers (150,000)
- Moderately Engaged Customers (150,000)
- Low Engagement Customers (150,000)

Each customer group is broken into three 'like' groups by using a random select, splitting each into groups of 50,000 customers. The test matrix would be as follows:

Segment Code	Segment Type	Quantity	Marketing	Total Transactions	Avg Transactions	Total Revenue	Avg Revenue
1	Highly Engaged	50,000	Loyalty Rich				
2	Highly Engaged	50,000	Loyalty Moderate				
3	Highly Engaged	50,000	No Program				
	Total	150,000					
4	Moderately Engaged	50,000	Loyalty Rich				
5	Moderately Engaged	50,000	Loyalty Moderate				
6	Moderately Engaged	50,000	No Program				
	Total	150,000					
7	Low Engagement	50,000	Loyalty Rich				
8	Low Engagement	50,000	Loyalty Moderate				
9	Low Engagement	50,000	No Program				
	Total	150,000					

Note that on average the customer groups in segments 1-3 are identical. The same is true for segments 4-6 and 7-9.

The quantity of each cell could vary based on the size of the customer base and objectives in testing. Also, as noted, the more engaged customer groups can be tested using lower quantities than the less engaged groups. Statistical validity testing can be used to determine appropriate quantities.

The program would be offered to customers using direct marketing. Customers in each group would be exposed to the test marketing while a group of like customers – referred to as the **Control Group** – would not receive the program marketing and associated benefits (Marketing = No Program).

The activity of customers in each group would be measured from the day of the program test launch. Results would be read after one month, two months, three, etc. The key metric is the average revenue and the question to answer is this: *Does the contribution from incremental revenue offset incremental costs and create more profitability for the brand? If so, which customer segments create the most profitability?*

NOTE that when measuring trends for each segment within customer segment type – in this example Highly, Moderately, Low – in the months just prior to the test, all metrics of the test and corresponding control groups should be very similar. If this is not the case, there are flaws in the randomization of splitting the customers into multiple groups which negate the ability to measure properly. You can check this after building the segmentation but before launching the test.

Based on results, the winning marketing program would be rolled out to customer segments which demonstrated acceptable return on investment.

Testing when individualized customer data is NOT available

This situation is common for traditional retailers who have brick-and-mortar locations. Multi-channel retailers typically track online sales to individual customers, but without reasons to provide an identifier at brick-and-mortar point of sale, many retail and entertainment brands such as theatre chains are not able to track individual customers.

In this situation, testing is best done at a metro-market level. What that means is that stores in metropolitan markets are compared based on overall sales, transaction counts, transaction size, etc. The markets usually include the total metro areas associated with a city. Two or more metro areas that typically have consistent purchase and revenue trends are identified. The program is then tested in market(s) and the comparable markets are used for measurement – or **Control Markets**.

The results will be less robust with this test method, but overall results can be measured, and feedback will be generated to refine the marketing tactics.

MIKE CASE

Suppose, for example, a company operates in all fifty states and we are testing ONE program structure. Analysis indicates that the stores in these cities trend similarly:

Dallas and Houston; Philadelphia and Pittsburgh; San Francisco and Seattle

Market	Marketing	Total Transactions	Avg Transactions	Total Revenue	Avg Revenue
Dallas Stores	Loyalty Program				
Houston Stores	No Loyalty Program				
Philadelphia Stores	Loyalty Program				
Pittsburgh Stores	No Loyalty Program				
San Francisco Stores	Loyalty Program				
Seattle Stores	No Loyalty Program				

Online customers located in the test regions would be served the marketing online based on cookies obtained during prior purchases, an IP address, or when they identify their location at checkout.

The total market level activity of all customers would be measured from the day of the program test launch by comparing average metrics per store. Again, results would be read after one month, two months, three, etc. The key here is to collect information to answer this: *Does the contribution from incremental revenue offset incremental costs and create more profitability for the brand?*

Again, the metrics in these markets in the months <u>just prior</u> to the test should track in very consistent trends.

Based on results, the program would be rolled out to additional markets or refinements made and additional testing performed.

The critical importance of testing

In the fall of 2011, Ron Johnson was appointed as not just the CEO of JC Penney, but as the savior responsible for energizing a brand that had been struggling in recent years. Seventeen months later, he was out of a job. While several mistakes were made, there is one thing that would have averted the biggest disaster in the brand's more than 100-year history.

While with Apple, Johnson is credited as the force that turned the Apple store into a huge success story. JC Penny had long appealed to middle America and had used proven retail tactics including sales and discount coupons to drive traffic. Their clientele tended to be older and valued this approach.

Johnson wanted to reinvent JC Penney as a hip brand with appeal to millennials – which of course sounds great. To accomplish this, they changed the apparel, removed several store brands and eliminated sales and targeted discount coupons. They launched the 'new' JC Penney and quickly found out that their new younger target customer had no affinity with JC Penney and that was not going to change overnight. At the same time, they alienated their long-term customers, who abandoned them in droves and were quickly captured by Kohls and other retail brands.

Revenue plummeted, but Johnson believed the change would just take time and stayed the course. As I said, he was ousted within seventeen months of joining the company. JC Penney's stock price was $32 when Johnson came on board and had been as high as $85 in the prior four years. As of this writing it trades at less than $2. While the brand had other challenges to overcome, this catastrophic collapse could have been avoided.

Johnson and the team launched the radically new marketing and store concepts across the entire chain without any tests. Setting up test and control markets to measure results first would have quickly set things on a better course. Unfortunately, this was not done and by the time JC Penney reverted to their tried-and-true approach they had lost countless customers they would never get back. For a struggling brand this was a blow from which they may never recover. Shareholders lost millions and employees lost jobs.

Test first...

Should you track engagement metrics?

Yes.

Customer metrics such as website visits, email open and click rates, and social media interactions are indicators of how engaged customers are with your brand. If these metrics are trending up, this would be a good thing.

A trend in recent years is for consultants to coach clients toward relying on these indicators to measure brand health and overall marketing performance. Marketing leaders often gravitate to these strategies, which can be good barometers if used correctly. These metrics should move in a consistent trend with customer revenue. But this is not always the case.

Revenue First

A goal of reading this book might be increasing your ability to design and execute marketing strategy to achieve the goals set by senior management and ownership.

As it turns out, customer revenue growth – at least of dramatic proportions – is likely to be the most difficult metric to improve.

Let's consider an email communications manager. For this role, success metrics should include improving email open and click-through rates. However, some strategies used to do this may be in direct conflict to a goal of maximizing total customer revenue. This is true as well of SMS and other push communications.

Let's assume you have a position selling goods for an online business and manage email communications. You test into a short-term, 5-day (Monday thru Friday) 'sale'. This email and offer are quite effective in obtaining very high open, click-through, and purchases when you send the initial email on Monday.

If your primary goal is maximizing engagement metrics, this is a major step toward your goal, and you should move on to the next campaign. In practice, however, this is what you should do:

Re-mail the same customer group the '5-day sale' notification again on Thursday with a 'last chance, offer ends soon' message. While most of the customers interested in the offer would have already taken advantage, many may have missed the first email, procrastinated, or were contemplating what they may be interested in initially and forgot about it.

What you would expect when re-mailing a 'last chance' reminder for the offer is to obtain about half of the open, clicks, and click-through revenue you obtained when you sent the initial email. From an engagement standpoint, this would lower your overall averages. However, if the buy-through rate was high on the initial email, even at half of that total the email should generate strong brand revenue and is the right step toward driving the most important metric: customer revenue growth to fuel the growth of the overall brand.

There are countless examples of this. You may email sweepstakes offers or online games for opening emails or providing information. These often have improved open rates but poor buy-through purchase rates. Some customers open with no intention of buying and customers who may have been influenced to purchase with a strong, highly-personalized, relevant product message become distracted by the tactic and do not purchase.

So, by <u>not</u> sending the follow-up 'sale' email or by aggressively sending game/sweeps tactics you can drive up 'engagement metrics' per email sent. But company revenue may actually decline.

I have seen these dynamics at several large organizations and coached CMOs on the dangers of reliance on engagement metrics without proper focus and science in place to track revenue.

So, track revenue while focusing on increasing engagement metrics which lead to goal one: increased revenue.

Launching a new marketing initiative

If you are working with a brand that has customer-facing employees or service representatives, they often prove critical for success. You may have the most uniquely designed marketing initiative ever created, but your first question is not just will the marketplace embrace it, it's will the <u>internal</u> team embrace it.

At La Quinta Inn & Suites, once our measurements had proven the changes in marketing were effective among Returns members, our next challenge was motivating our teammates at the properties. Most program enrollments happened at the hotels when guests checked in for their stays, so we depended on the hotel teams to drive enrollments.

We designed a Returns Program enrollment promotion which would be run multiple times each year. They were designed to motivate the regional leadership, hotel general managers, and front desk service representatives. Key elements for any promotion should include:

- Regular communications
- Create competitions within the team and report regularly on results
- Above all else, do everything possible to make it tremendous fun

We grouped geographic regions into five subgroups each with similar enrollment activity based on their enrollment levels before the promotion. The region who won in each subgroup received a cash prize for the leader to use to reward or celebrate with their team.

Each property was given an enrollment goal designed to increase their current enrollment levels. If the property reached their goal, all front service desk representatives with at least five enrollments during the promotion received a gift card.

The data showed that some service reps were both good at enrolling <u>and</u> were actively promoting the program, while others had few enrollments. Setting a goal for the entire property ensured that strong representatives would work with and coach less-active representatives to ensure overall success. Since each property had a unique stretch goal, the cost justification economics of their rewards were assured if they reached their goal.

We kicked things off with: ***The Enrollment League***

We used a superhero theme patterned on DC Comics' *Justice League of America*. Since the promotion was internal and not customer-facing, copyrights were not an issue. In fact, while the real Justice League were characters from only DC Comics, we used the best superheroes from both DC and Marvel since, for this purpose, we could.

We sent posters for weekly tracking of results toward the six-week goals and encouraged general managers to post them for employee viewing in break rooms. When we started the promotions, our Human Resource group laughed at me, saying few would comply with hanging the posters. I love a challenge, and this attitude just further motivated our team.

Our marketing to the general managers stated that if they took a picture of their poster up at the property and emailed it to us, we would put them in for a drawing for movie tickets for the whole team. This element was almost an afterthought, but it proved very powerful.

The results proved something I had learned working with brands throughout the years: set up a fun theme with a competitive group of people and don't be surprised when they go the extra mile.

Soon, we started receiving pictures of the posters. But not just of the posters and not just a few pictures -- we received hundreds of photos from properties all over North America. Most properties were also staging pictures of the posters that included their staffs. Many dressed up as superheroes. One property let their team create their own unique superheroes patterned after La Quinta's core values. Another property sent a picture each week that, when complete, told a mini-story of La Quinta triumphing over our evil archenemies – the competitive hotel brands.

MIKE CASE

The pictures provided powerful material we used in weekly follow-up emails to the teams (remember, communicate regularly). General managers who were not actively participating saw their peers fully engaged and inspiring amazing engagement. Each week, a larger percentage of the properties got engaged. The results? The highest six-week enrollment numbers in company history, a record we went on to beat many times in subsequent promotions.

With so many powerful images of engagement from the properties we created a short video we deemed a 'movie'. We sent movie premier posters to the properties and encouraged them to view the video using an online link. Many General Managers held movie watching parties for their teams.

CUSTOMER DEVOTION

CUSTOMER SEGMENTATION

Congratulations! You have done the strategic work of designing, testing, and implementing a loyalty program. This is a significant milestone. However, your work is not done, in fact, it may only be beginning.

This has been a common debate with colleagues over the years. What percentage of true success is due to the design and implementation versus executing, testing, and continual innovative refinement? The easy answer is 50% for each. Having taken over loyalty marketing for numerous brands, I believe that an even higher percentage of success is dependent on the execution. That being said a successful program design will fail if not executed properly and a flawed design fails even with good execution.

Understanding customer segments is important

Unique customer segments behave in unique ways. Customers in transactional businesses should be placed into segments in order to effectively market to them and measure the results of marketing efforts. This is conceptually the same for a subscription business where customers within the first one-three months of tenure have the highest attrition rates.

Segmentation is just as important as you execute marketing as when new marketing programs are designed and launched. Within the umbrella of the marketing program you should continually be testing messaging, promotional offers, and enhanced services to customers. Customer segments often do not respond in the same way. Well-structured tests allow you to selectively optimize retention efforts to maximize incremental customer revenue.

The RFM model is one of the keys here. In traditional, transaction-based businesses your most **R**ecent and **F**requent customers will be the most likely to purchase from you again – and the most likely to respond to relevant communications or promotions to encourage another purchase. Depending on the business, other variables should be included as well.

To facilitate robust testing, you segment customers into groups. You then develop ongoing CRM campaigns, offers, promotions, or even relationship communications and test a variety to each group. In this way you can increase the odds that you will find the communication streams and customer group combinations which maximize overall results.

As an example, we'll assume a simple segmentation of customers into three groups. In practice, there would be more than three, but whether there are three, five, or twenty-five segments, the methodology is the same. Let's also assume we want to test two promotional offers against no-offer communications. For this example, we have 600,000 customers which split evenly into equal thirds per customer segment.

The communications matrix would look like this:

Segment Code	Segment Type	Quantity	Marketing	Total Transactions	Avg Transactions	Total Revenue	Avg Revenue
1	New Customers	50,000	Offer 1 Rich				
2	New Customers	50,000	Offer 2 Moderate				
3	New Customers	100,000	Communication Only				
	Total	200,000					
4	Stay Awhile Customers	50,000	Offer 1 Rich				
5	Stay Awhile Customers	50,000	Offer 2 Moderate				
6	Stay Awhile Customers	100,000	Communication Only				
	Total	200,000					
7	Tenured Customers	25,000	Offer 1 Rich				
8	Tenured Customers	25,000	Offer 2 Moderate				
9	Tenured Customers	150,000	Communication Only				
	Total	200,000					

You may find that one offer achieves highest ROI with New Customers, the other offer with Stay Awhiles, and communications only with Tenured customers -- or any other combination. But with this approach, you have multiple chances for a positive outcome. If the promotional offers are not successful among any customer segment you also have key learnings – which is in itself a positive outcome.

Testing, however, is not all about promotional offers. You could and should run the same types of tests for the creative and messaging in the communications. Your goal is to be relevant to unique customer segments. This is accomplished in the same way, using the same illustrative example, by substituting 'Messaging 1' and 'Messaging 2' for the promotional offers. This is where many brands fail. The messaging for a tenured customer who purchases one type of product should be distinctly different from that for new customers purchasing another type of product. There is no one size fits all, or most, customers when trying to achieve significant revenue growth.

As a last point, be aware that you should not test more than one key variable at a time. You would not do a key messaging test with an offer against the control messaging. If the test won, you would not know if it was the messaging or offer which drove the result. You would test this combination in this way:

Segment Code	Segment Type	Quantity	Marketing	Total Transactions	Avg Transactions	Total Revenue	Avg Revenue
1	New Customers	50,000	Offer Test - cntl message				
2	New Customers	50,000	Message Test 1				
3	New Customers	100,000	Control Message				
	Total	200,000					

<u>This process for testing is ongoing</u>. As your brand begins having results increasing customer revenue your competitors should be working diligently to reverse that trend. With a dynamic marketplace your work is never done as you continually explore innovated communication streams and offers.

What customer promotional offer works best?

This is another question I've been asked by senior leadership. The answer to this question should be based on the ROI achieved with the promotional offer, since most offers involve a cost or revenue dilution. Odds are very high there is no single best offer that works best with ALL program members or customers. If there is, the business is either in a unique situation or, more likely, not approaching data-driven marketing efforts in the most effective manner.

For a transactional business you would set the communication objectives based on customer activity:

After a customer's first transaction

As we know, there are challenges with new customers. In order to motivate a second transaction from new customers, the timing of communications is as critical as the content. You will want to communicate quickly and in a manner that is perceived as sincere. Sure, most companies trigger some type of email when you purchase from them, but that alone does not begin to accomplish our goals. You want to begin creating a personalized relationship with a unique personality. You also may need incentives to help drive the all-important second transaction.

Ongoing Relationship

Once you get the second transaction it becomes easier – but never easy. You then need to cultivate the relationship to get the third, fourth, and so on. At some point, the customer begins to have the characteristics of a 'best' customer. Analytics will show you at what point this becomes true for your business. At some point, the percentage of customer attrition after a transaction will start to become flat. For example, after eight transactions the percentage who make ninth, tenth, etc. will become somewhat similar.

During this stage of the customer lifecycle before the customer reaches a 'steady-state' point for your business, you should be testing messaging and offers aggressively.

<u>Maintaining Loyalty</u>

Once a customer reaches a certain point, they might advance to a top tier of your program and have enhanced benefits. Beyond this, you would typically only selectively make promotional offers which can have substantial cost. If their behavior changes and they have not been back in a reasonable timeframe, you might make an aggressive offer.

For these customers, recognizing them at all touch points is critical and is low-cost. Thanking them for their business in a manner perceived as sincere is also highly effective.

Customer Communications

As you read this, you may be someone who has or had a role with responsibility for customer communications. Or, at a minimum, you probably have done business with brands who now send you emails, mail, text messaging, and other direct communications based on having identified you and having your contact information.

I sign up for all the customer programs I encounter. Regardless of my intention to use the brand again, I am always curious about what brands are doing to maximize long-term customer revenue.

In many cases what I see - even from established legacy companies in travel – is that companies do not effectively execute customized communications for the recipients. Many brands – even those with established CRM programs – seem to have little or no communications strategy at all.

What happens with many brands is that customer databases become thought of as the well to go to as often as possible if revenue is down, a revenue target is in jeopardy, or to get rid of excess inventory. When this is the case customers – even loyalty members – are bombarded with 'sales' for goods or services to purchase regardless of the customer's likelihood to have interest in the goods or even if the customer has not bought the most popular items in years.

With little relevance, customers can stop opening email. Over time, that means the email will go directly to the customer spam folder and not be seen. Or customers will simply unsubscribe, shrinking the marketable customer database – a vitally important asset for any company.

What to avoid

Companies with undifferentiated communications may justify their strategy with data points about email opt-out rates. It is true that many consumers will just keep deleting away emails for long periods of time without taking the time to remove themselves from the email lists.

But there is an important aspect to note about opt-out rates – or the number of customers removing themselves from your future communications. Whether a partner is sending or designing your messages, or even if the internal marketing group is reporting them, they often like to quote the number of customer opt-outs which occurred as a percentage of the entire group receiving the email. This is terribly misleading. Most recipients never <u>open</u> the email. And if the communication strategy is not engaging, the percentage opening the emails goes down further.

To illustrate, we'll use this example. A company sends 1,000,000 delivered emails. 15,000 customers opt out of the company's communications. The reporting says 1.5% of customers opt out. Depending on the brand, the recipient list, and other factors, this may not 'feel' too bad. However, reviewing the metric in this manner is very misleading. The measurement you want to track is the percentage of opt-outs among recipients who OPENED the email, thereby having the opportunity to opt out. Keep in mind that customers who just deleted or otherwise never opened the email never had the opportunity to opt out.

If, for example, the percentage of recipients who opened the email was 15% – 150,000 customers -- and 15,000 customers opted out, we now see that 10% of the customers who opened the email opted out, which is terrible.

The takeaway is to track the opt-outs against the customers opening emails. I've seen brands measuring this incorrectly more often than you may imagine.

Determining Communication Cadence

Frequency of purchase cycle should drive frequency of communications. High-value customers of cruise lines may purchase once or twice a year – every year. High-value grocery store customers purchase every week.

As discussed, many retailers who encounter revenue challenges begin emailing their customer list more frequently. The rationale is that emails are inexpensive to send – so no real cost. This is not really true. If you send too many emails to customers who are not frequent buyers, they begin to ignore them. This is easily measurable by tracking open and click-through rates – or worse yet, changes to unsubscribe rates – within each customer segment.. The customer database is a tremendously valuable asset. As customers become less engaged, the value of this asset diminishes. What this means is the perception of no/low cost of sending emails to customers simply is not true.

Best practice is to send communications to customers in a cadence that is optimized for their purchase behavior. Upon my arrival, I have never found this to be the case at a company I have worked with, either as a consultant or employee. Analysis and testing allow optimization of communication cadence by customer segment and improved results.

Unraveling strategies which have proven ineffective

When I joined La Quinta Inn & Suites, the broad tracking studies for hospitality programs done by independent third parties showed that La Quinta's Returns program ranked at the bottom of all hotel programs in terms of effectiveness. After completing a competitive analysis, it was clear to me the program itself was competitive. However, things clearly needed to change to drive member retention in a way that would materially grow the brand.

While we did not make material changes to the program structure, we did make tremendous changes to the way the program was managed – all informed by learnings from enhanced analytics. As we made changes and began creating more passionately loyal guests, we initiated additional customer listening efforts. These included selectively sending both offline and digital communications to groups of our highest-revenue member guests to let them know they could contact me at TalktoMike@lq.com. We let them know they could reach out to me anytime, for any reason involving La Quinta, be it good or bad. This provided tremendous feedback from our most frequent guests and with some help from the team, I sent a personal response back to every customer who contacted us.

The feedback was invaluable for making improvements across the brand, selectively at specific locations and to the Returns program.

MIKE CASE

When we started this effort, I fielded a number of complaints from frequent staying members who had been part of the program for years. They complained that they were not receiving the rich bonus point offers they had in the past.. The reality was that they should have never been receiving such rich and costly offers. How would I know this? By testing to these customer segments with control groups, of course. When receiving these complaints, we gave the members a small number of points, and more importantly, assured them we were committed to taking better care of them than any other hospitality company (something these members were already noticing).

In response to customer feedback regarding issues during their stay, we apologized, provided a small number of points, and ensured them no one would take care of them like the team at La Quinta. Additionally, when possible, we acted to make changes and then communicated this back to the guests.

With these efforts and improvements in relationship building across the board, our members became passionately loyal. To be an Elite member in the program a member needed to stay 25+ nights annually. Within just a few years, we quadrupled the number of members reaching this status and increased loyalty among countless other member guests. This of course significantly increased the revenue contribution from program members to dramatically grow the brand. The growth facilitated a successful - and lucrative - Initial Public Offering (IPO) to take the company public and benefit both LQ's owners and employees.

When is customer attrition not customer attrition?

Joining Sage Telecom in January 2005 as the marketing and customer insights leader, I quickly determined that customer acquisition was the company's number one opportunity. Founded in 1996 when local phone service was deregulated, Sage had launched a first-of-its-kind local phone service bundle concept which included long distance and other features. Sage offered these services at a discount versus the corporate providers of the monopoly-era Bell System – later acquired by AT&T and Verizon.

Sage had also benefited from an effective acquisition marketing creative design and strategy which, during their first eight years, converted AT&T customers and grew Sage to $350 million in annual revenue. By 2005, other competitors had copied the bundling strategy, the cable TV companies had begun offering local phone service, and Sage's approach for acquiring new customers was no longer effective. Beginning nine months before my arrival, Sage Telecom had gone from 100 straight months of total customer growth to a company declining in total customers each month at an alarming and accelerating rate.

As a subscription-based phone service provider, Sage had near-perfect customer data, so we started where you should always start when you have data: customer-level analysis.

Acquiring new customers is a different marketing discipline than retention, but the analysis techniques to understand opportunities are similar. During my initial months we developed, implemented and continually refined highly effective strategies. Each month we increased the number of new customers acquired. Within eighteen months we had increased the yield from acquisition efforts by 40%. With no increase in acquisition marketing budget, we were attracting 40% more new customers each month at the same overall cost.

As months went by, this had a dramatic effect on the business. With success on the customer acquisition front during a particularly difficult competitive climate, we increased our focus on customer retention, ultimately launching Sage Select. We reported monthly on key customer performance indicators, so it was surprising when the CFO came into my office one morning and told me that despite our efforts, customer attrition was rising.

The CFO carried a report which the founders had developed years earlier. The report tracked net customers each month in this manner:

	Number	% of Total	Variance vs. Prior Month	Variance vs. Same Month Prior Year
Total Customers at the beginning of the Month	#	%	#	#
+ New Customers Acquired	#	%	#	#
- Customers Cancelling Service	#	%	#	#
= Total Monthly Customers	#			

While the overall customer counts were once again growing, it was true that the percentage of total customers canceling service had gone up versus prior time periods as shown in the report. I tried to explain that, despite this report, customer attrition had actually gone DOWN as a result of our efforts. The CFO had a difficult time understanding how this could be true. So, we pulled the customer data to clearly illustrate that, yes, customer attrition was decreasing.

What key customer data variable do you think we used to show the true state of the business?

If your first thought was "recency" you are making great progress. Remember that we had dramatically increased the number of new customers the business was acquiring each month. This is good for any business.

We demonstrated the truth about the state of the business using customer segmentation based on the recency variable. Unless there are customer contracts in place, in a subscription business the highest attrition rates are always among new customers. The reasons are many. Their former provider proactively tries to win them back; they decide the service does not meet their expectations; or they were simply taking advantage of a promotional offer to try the service. Attrition was down in every customer segment while overall attrition had increased. The following illustration demonstrates how attrition can go up – when it is actually going down.

MIKE CASE

	Customer Composition Current Month	Customer Composition Same Month Prior Year	Segment Attrition Current Month	Segment Attrition Same Month Prior Year	Measure Customer Attrition By Segment
New Customers (1 - 3 Month)	10%	5%	15%	19%	⇐
Passive Customers (4 - 12 Month)	16%	10%	9%	11%	⇐
Maturing Customers (13 - 24 Month)	35%	25%	6%	8%	⇐
Long-term Customers (25+ Months)	39%	60%	3%	4%	⇐
Weighted Average Attrition Rate =			7.6%	7.4%	

The analysis proves that it is the composition of the customer base that is causing an increase in overall attrition rates. While dramatically increasing the yield from customer acquisition marketing we were also increasing the overall percentage of new customers. Since newer customers attrite at much higher rates that long-term customers, the overall attrition rate was increasing. However, within each customer segment defined by recency the attrition rate was going down.

From that point forward a report showing year-over-year attrition by recency segment was included in management reporting.

When measuring customer attrition it is important to track it at a customer segment level. This provides substantially more insight into the state of the business when it comes to customer revenue.

Most Businesses' Reality – Finite Budgets

When embarking on a journey that leads to successful customer retention, there is typically a constraint that must be part of the planning process. Marketing budgets are usually finite — i.e. there is a limited amount of funds to spend on all efforts. How the overall budget is divided can be determined by many factors, but in the end the funds you can spend toward maximizing the lifetime value of customers have restrictions.

If the company is introducing a new customer loyalty initiative, then funds necessary to support the program typically come from reducing other efforts. Testing retention marketing limits financial risk and provides the results necessary to convince management to shift funds from other marketing or non-marketing areas. Smart organizations will demand data-driven proof of results before making significant investments. Ultimately, marketing costs must translate into increased customer revenue. If you had unlimited funds, you might focus the best-practice marketing and customer service at all customers equally. However, this will not be the case.

Customer data has been widely available for decades, and the depth of the data has grown very rapidly in recent years. Interestingly, however, when it comes to customer level marketing and customer care, it is not uncommon for brands to spend resources against customers in a relatively equal manner.

Success is highly dependent upon two key objectives:

1. Identifying which new customers offer the greatest long-term revenue potential and spending specifically and appropriately against them.
2. Managing your most valuable customers in a way that ensures you retain them more effectively than your competitors do.

This is accomplished by shifting resources and spending <u>away</u> from low revenue potential customers to highest revenue potential newly acquired and demonstrated value existing customers.

Real world examples

We've covered a number of examples which demonstrate engineered strategies to accomplish uniquely specific company objectives. I'll share another to help conceptualize customer segmentation goals.

Although La Quinta Inn & Suites serves as this example, the goals are generic for travel providers who serve guests traveling for both work and leisure reasons and are widely published in travel industry publications.

La Quinta opened their first hotel in 1968, and by the 2000s had grown to over 800 locations in the US, Mexico, and Canada, with annual revenue well over $1 billion. Hospitality is generally categorized as 'full service' (high-end hotels with restaurants and bars), 'mid-service' (typically catering to both business and leisure travelers), and 'no service' (brands such as Motel 6 and many small independently-owned brands).

CUSTOMER DEVOTION

La Quinta competes in the mid-service category, offering comfortable rooms with free high-speed internet and free breakfast. Competing with brands such as Hampton Inn & Suites from Hilton, Fairfield from Marriott and Comfort Inn & Suites, La Quinta provides accommodations for both business travel and guests traveling for pleasure.

Some considerations:

<u>When</u>

People traveling for work are most likely to stay at a hotel on weeknights (Monday – Thursday), allowing them to return to their homes for weekends. People traveling for pleasure are most likely to travel over a weekend or nights which include weekend nights.

<u>Where</u>

Traveler's work destinations are often different than the destinations travelers choose for leisure travel. With some allowance for the nights of the week stayed and season of stay, travelers to destinations such as Clearwater Beach Florida or California's gold coast wine country would seem to be more likely to be leisure travelers than people staying in Waco, Texas or Harrisburg, Pennsylvania.

<u>How often</u>

A travel/hospitality provider's goal should be building tremendous relationships with travelers. More importantly, the goal should be building true Customer Devotion among travelers who travel OFTEN – those travelers who spend 20, 40, 80 nights or more each year at hotels.

While there are exceptions, people who travel for work-related reasons – on average – will travel more total days/nights each year than those traveling exclusively for leisure. Most business travelers, to a lesser degree, also travel for leisure, making them even more valuable long-term guests.

This probably seems obvious. And since most travel companies have good customer tracking data, exploring this type of hypothesis through customer analytics is not difficult.

While in practice there are other variables that indicate high-value potential customers in the travel industry, for simplicity we'll consider only these two attributes: Which day(s) of the week a new customer's stay takes place and where.

Imagine that during a week you have 2,000 newly-acquired customers stay at a mid-service hotel brand serving business and leisure travelers. Assume 1,000 of them stayed on or during a Monday through Thursday and 1,000 stayed during Friday – Sunday.

If we knew nothing else, it would seem a logical bet that the potential future revenue value for the brand is higher for the 1,000 customers staying on mid-week nights. And remember, as a hospitality provider with excellent customer level data, an analysis of newly-acquired customers in prior months would prove or disprove this hypothesis.

You then overlay the geographic location of the customer stays to further refine the segmentation.

Many travel brands attempt to sign up travelers into their loyalty programs, then typically send them both digital and offline physical communications. This often results in spending finite budgets evenly across customer segments.

By shifting finite resources and budget away from lower revenue potential leisure travelers and potentially doubling the efforts against likely business travelers, the result over time can be an exponential increase in the 'yield' of the marketing efforts. Converting a higher percentage of customers with higher lifetime revenue values results in higher customer revenue over time from the same marketing spend.

The reason for this is simple. Assuming these are business travelers but that this is their first visit to your brand, and knowing that business travelers typically travel frequently, it's a safe bet that these travelers most often stay with another brand.

Your goal as a marketer is to reinforce the guest's reasons for choosing your brand this first time (free amenities, convenient locations, great value, etc.) and to convince the traveler you are their best option going forward.

Converting one of these business travelers to your brand is worth significantly more than one of the leisure travelers, who may on average stay 2-6 nights a year at hotels. This gives business travelers a higher average life time value - often 10X+. By creating preference for your brand among a larger percentage of these customers, the brand can increase long term revenue from new customers exponentially.

In the example above, now consider that the 2,000 newly-acquired customers happens every day, 365 days a year. You are now more effectively communicating to hundreds of thousands of your new customers at no incremental cost. Each week, influencing a higher percentage of these high-value travelers to have a second stay significantly increases the chances they stay a third time. Each time you continue to build 'purchase habit' and, if the brand has enrolled the traveler in a loyalty program, the guests continue earning benefits which create a tangible value – or opportunity cost - to bring them back for a fourth, fifth, and beyond stay.

Week in and week out, your marketing spend is more effective. Over time, it results in customer revenue which grows significantly.

Similar analogies exist in most consumer categories. Determine the attributes of higher LTV potential customers after their very first purchase and use the information to tailor marketing efforts to generate customer revenue growth over time.

RETENTION BEGINS WITH CUSTOMER ACQUISITION

Customer retention full circle

If you have not already, at some point you may hear "effective customer retention starts with customer acquisition." There is truth in this. Having encountered and overcome the leaking bucket analogy a number of times, it has become clear to me that enhanced customer acquisition efforts must be part of any significant revenue growth equation.

Once we made headway understanding customer segments and focused marketing to measurably retain high-value customers, the next step was clear: use the data insights from high LTV customers to create new, focused, data-driven customer acquisition strategies.

This is how you get there:

When you have effective customer segmentation driving CRM strategies, you should have data-driven insights on key customer segments as well as their lifetime values. All brands, or nearly all, have certain customer segments who tend to transact more often and over a longer period of time.

Profiling most-profitable customer segments with both data and quantitative research provides you with demographic and psychographic insights into these customers. While it is interesting to hypothesize why certain customer segments are more profitable over time, the bottom line is this: once your analysis has identified customer segments that are statistically proven to be more valuable over time, your acquisition efforts should evolve to attract more customers fitting these profiles.

If you are working with a new or rapidly-expanding business, this may be a moving target as you continue to rapidly acquire new customer types. However, while working with startups I have found that as you acquire new customers you very quickly have enough data for the initial definition of these segments.

Locating Future High-Value Customers

An important step in the customer profiling process is locating exactly where these customer segments reside. While the following analytic approach achieves this goal in the US, I have used the same approach in developed countries around the world.

Step one: profile recently acquired new customers.

In the United States this is done by looking at a recent set of new customers and identifying the zip codes where they reside. You can get more highly refined results by using zip code + 4 for greater accuracy. Zip code can be <u>any</u> geographic designator and therefore translates to using other geographic identifiers in the US as well as in other parts of the world.

For the analysis, there must be enough time after the customers were acquired to determine their long-term value. This can vary widely by industry or product, but with typical goods or services this can often be done within 60 to 120 days after the customer's first transaction. Keep in mind that for a transactional business, a significant indicator of longer-term value is the second transaction alone, while in a subscription business it is typically a customer maintaining the subscription through the first 3 or 4 months.

Once the analysis is completed, you assign a value for low-value new customers versus high-value new customers. In many transactional businesses, low-value new customers would include single transaction customers during the analysis timeframe (60 days, 90 days, 180 days, etc.). Higher-value customers may be defined as 2+, 3+, 4+, etc. transactions. If the distribution of revenue for each transaction is significant, then you would use total revenue collected from customers to score their value.

Use a distribution of transactions during the initial months of a customer's relationship with your brand to determine low- versus high-value potential. From a simplicity standpoint it often makes sense to start with a simple approach and use only two outcomes to rank customers as 'low' or 'high' value. You then assign new customer values as follows:

Low-value new customers are assigned a value of '1'.

High-value new customers are assigned a value of '3'.

You can of course weight new customer value more precisely for low versus high by using customer revenue from the analysis. With this approach, weighting ultra-high-value customers even more highly would improve prospective customer scoring.

Now sum the scores of all customers within each defined geographic area, which in this case is zip code or zip code + 4.

Seems simple enough, right? But population size means each zip code is not 'equal'. Zip codes with significantly higher population density end up with higher overall scores since you are likely to have acquired more customers from these more densely populated areas. The next step is to obtain the total population, or ideally the total households, for each geographic area defined. Population information within the United States is readily available and can often be downloaded at no cost or obtained with inexpensive software. The data is similarly available for most economically-developed countries worldwide.

New Customer Lifetime Value Index

At this point you have two important pieces of information:

1. A cumulative customer score for each zip code
2. Total population (or households) for each zip code

Dividing total cumulative customer score by total households creates an index for each zip code. With this simple calculation you have now created a *New Customer Lifetime Value Index* for each geographic area. Importantly, the index is not just determining the areas where you acquire the most new customers, it pinpoints <u>where you are getting the highest individual customer lifetime value</u>.

Now rank order the geographic regions by *New Customer Lifetime Value Index* highest to lowest.

This begins to help pinpoint where customer acquisition marketing and sales efforts should be targeted as well as which geographic areas to shift efforts away from.

There are going to be high LTV customers in every region and to the extent you can target them precisely using direct marketing, you could continue to do so in low average new customer LTV areas. However, for the mass marketing efforts often used for acquisition, shifting focus will net a higher return. If done correctly, this is always true because, statistically, customers acquired from high LTV areas on average have significantly higher revenue than customers from low LTV areas.

Los Angeles is a highly populated metro area where many brands market products and services. Executing marketing to create awareness and trial throughout greater Los Angeles is an expensive proposition. However, pin pointing the specific areas within LA that result in most of the customer revenue allows marketers to concentrate efforts and significantly increase the return of acquisition marketing. Los Angeles has over 4 million residents and 98 zip codes. Using the approach outlined allows you to increase focus on very specific areas within the metro area to yield improved results. Illustratively the analysis would result in something like the following - allowing marketers to begin making more informed decisions regarding acquisition marketing:

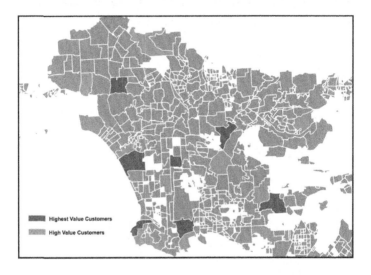

There is an easy argument for why you will want to refine the analysis over time.

"Neighbors living right next door to each other may have very different lifestyles."

For example, one neighbor may be a young couple with multiple children and in the next house you may have a retired couple who never had children. Consumer needs and values are no doubt different in these two households.

However, on average, you will find that areas where your most profitable customers tend to be concentrated are where you will find new similarly highly profitable customers. With this data alone, most organizations can dramatically improve customer acquisition efforts. Where available, you would use as much insight as possible to target customer marketing efforts. From here you move to the next step.

Further Refinement of Acquisition targeting

In the previous example, we assigned individual new customers a value index of 1 or 3. This was done using internal or primary data and is the most important step you will take. With this in place, the next step is to overlay these customers with demographic data.

You may need to use an external data service provider to overlay demographic variables at the customer level. Demographic data at an individual customer or household level is readily available from large providers including Experian, Equifax, and Transunion, either directly or through many secondary client service providers. This type of data append for analysis purposes can be done at a low cost. There are 100+ potential demographic data variables available at the individual person or household level.

The demographic overlay variables which are most typically predictive of consumer behavior include:

- Gender
- Age
- Household Income
- Home ownership vs. renter

- Value of home
- Presence of child or children in the home
- Age of child or children
- Education level

There are many other variables available and during the analysis most should be used to eliminate hunches as to which variables will be predictive.

Now we proceed to the next step of the analysis.

Within your target zip codes set an index of 100 for each variable, based on the average presence of each variable among <u>all households</u> in the zip code. For example, if 25% of the population in your target area is over 65, then the index of 100 is based on 25% being this age. Your <u>customers</u> within each zip code are then collectively assigned an index for the same variables. From here your analysis identifies which variables index significantly higher, or lower, than the averages for the population in the target zip codes. The result could look something like this:

CUSTOMER DEVOTION

New Customer Index

Demographic Variable	Universe Index	Customers Acquired Index
Gender		
Male	100	93
Female	100	106
Age		
Under 30	100	82
30 - 44	100	85
45 - 64	100	94
65 +	100	165
Education		
Less Than HS	100	120
High School	100	140
Some College	100	110
College Degree	100	72
Masters Degree	100	50
Etc.,		

You want to see at least 10 points of differentiation to conclude that the variable is predictive. The higher the variance is to the 100 index indicates stronger correlation for the variable – be it positive or negative. In this example, we conclude that gender is not a predictive variable for buying our product. With a significant over index for residents 65+ and under index for residents 44 and younger we would target older prospects. Lastly, over-indexing among prospects without college degrees allows further targeting insight.

Traditional acquisition marketing

Many companies have marketing divided at a macro level as:

- Brand marketing or new customer acquisition
- Retention marketing

There are instances where this may make a lot of sense. Traditional branding/acquisition marketing is a different science than retention marketing and driven by uniquely different goals. The primary - and secondary - goal of brand marketing and less-targeted marketing efforts should be attracting new customers. If you have customer-level data and can communicate directly with customers, then there may be no instance when you would use mass marketing for anything but customer acquisition.

Marketing done to expose consumers to the brand and encourage trial is often done through less targeted channels and with less data to influence the targeting of messages.

Having access to customer-level data allows for targeted retention efforts through much more cost efficient, direct-to-the-customer marketing channels. Additionally, the messaging for customer acquisition and retention marketing should be different. New customers have either pre-conceived or no perceptions about your brand. Existing customers have experienced the brand and formed perceptions.

While this may seem obvious, I once had a CMO for a brand struggling with customer acquisition explain to me that a material goal of their mass marketing was retention. The brand had individualized customer data and a structured loyalty program. In this case a goal involving retention for mass marketing efforts was terribly flawed and the acquisition results reflected these problems.

If there are resources dedicated to new customer acquisition, their efforts are often either:

1. Not measured at all
2. Measured using engagement metrics
3. Measured by the total number of new customers acquired. This would typically be benchmarked versus results from the same calendar timeframe during the prior year.

No surprise I favor the third benchmark, but it is more complicated than this.

What if the total newly acquired customer totals go down?

More profitable new customers are often harder to acquire and may have a higher cost per acquisition. This can be true because high-value customers are actively purchasing in the category with competitors who should be using their own CRM efforts to retain them. For this reason, lower-value new customers often have a lower cost to acquire. Most acquisition models unfortunately do not take this into account and therefore may be optimized toward acquiring a high number of low-value customers.

The number one metric for all marketing – customer revenue – often yields a much different approach than acquisition models optimized on new customer volume designed to minimize cost per acquisition. Using new customer LTV will shift spending away from low-value to higher-value customers. A result of this may be that the total <u>number</u> of new customers acquired goes down.

Since in most cases acquisition marketing is measured by customers acquired, having this metric go down is something no one is happy with. But it may not be a bad thing – and if the number of new customers with high-value customer profiles is going up, the result can be exceedingly positive.

The customer revenue decile analysis is likely to indicate that the average customer LTV of the top 30% of customers (or top 3 revenue deciles) has a revenue value 10 to 20 times higher than the bottom 30% of customers. For this example, we will use a conservative value of approximately 10 times the revenue value. Using the benchmark of every 100 customers acquired, consider this:

Current Acquisition Marketing

Revenue Decile	Customers Acquired	% of Total	12 Month Revenue	Current State Revenue
1	10	10.0%	$185	$1,850
2	10	10.0%	$80	$800
3	10	10.0%	$58	$580
4	10	10.0%	$41	$410
5	10	10.0%	$36	$360
6	10	10.0%	$28	$280
7	10	10.0%	$22	$220
8	10	10.0%	$17	$170
9	10	10.0%	$14	$140
10	10	10.0%	$10	$100
Total	100			$4,910

Optimized Acquisition Marketing

Revenue Decile	Customers Acquired	% of Total	12 Month Revenue	Optimized State Marketing
1	12	13.0%	$185	$2,220
2	13	14.1%	$80	$1,040
3	14	15.2%	$58	$812
4	10	10.9%	$41	$410
5	10	10.9%	$36	$360
6	10	10.9%	$28	$280
7	10	10.9%	$22	$220
8	5	5.4%	$17	$85
9	4	4.3%	$14	$56
10	4	4.3%	$10	$40
Total	92			$5,523

Variance of Optimized Marketing

Variance	Numbers	Percentage
Customers	8	-8.0%
Revenue	$613	12.5%

New customers acquired decreases by 8% while total revenue from newly-acquired customers during their first 12 months increases by 12.5%. If we were to consider 24 months, the new customer revenue increase would be even greater.

If, as a marketer, you can implement these strategies and increase the revenue yield of acquisition marketing by nearly 13% with the same budget, prepare for a promotion, raise, bonus, or all three. If these do not occur, find a place to work where they will truly appreciate your professional talents – you will find there are many.

The leaky bucket reimagined

During my career as we successfully implemented these strategies, it became clear it was time to make an addition to the leaking bucket illustration.

Your goal is to optimize acquisition efforts to get more high-value new customers and fewer low-value new customers. The bright blue water represents high-value customers, the murky water low-value customers. When you get here, hold on! Dramatic revenue growth ensues.

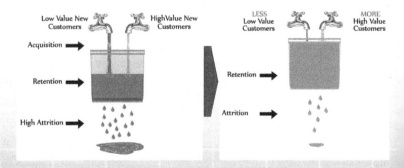

The acquisition engine alone does not maximize long term growth

This was the case early in my career, when I joined First USA Bank, one of the US's leading Visa/MasterCard issuers.

During the 1980s, the founders of First USA purchased the small credit card portfolio of a failing bank in Texas. They incorporated the new company in Wilmington, Delaware and set about marketing nationally to acquire new card members.

First USA was one of the early financial institutions to adopt a model of selling banking products exclusively through direct marketing channels. The company marketed First USA bankcards with the acceptance associations of both Visa and MasterCard. Using this model of selling exclusively through direct marketing channels, not physical banking locations, First USA quickly became one of the fastest growing bankcard issuers in the country. In a short timeframe, through the early to late 1990s, First USA grew from the 14th largest issuer in the country to the 3rd largest issuer.

It was one thing to see First USA overcome big regional banks such as Key Bank, but its eventual growth to become larger than Chase, Bank of America, Wells Fargo, and other giant banking brands was astounding.

First USA's move to accelerate growth

Having built a customer acquisition engine which may have had no rival during the 1990s, First USA was acquiring new cardmembers from larger competitive banks at a dizzying rate. While growing quickly, they realized that even a moderate amount of customer attrition against a large and growing customer base represented a tremendous amount of lost revenue.

First USA's next move was to create a newly defined cardmember loyalty leadership position and they began seeking candidates. I was working in the American Airlines AAdvantage group, developing and launching international partnerships. With this background, First USA offered me this new role of building strategies and launching loyalty initiatives to increase customer life time value.

Despite becoming a large company, First USA operated with an entrepreneurial mindset that closely measured risk and encouraged aggressive testing at a rapid pace. My team developed and launched dozens of targeted strategies that increased the value of our product for customers and significantly reduced cardmember attrition.

The combination of highly effective customer acquisition marketing along with a customer base that continually became more loyal allowed First USA to become the fastest-growing bankcard issuer in North America. This growth eventually facilitated a lucrative buy-out by a large traditional bank.

The shareholders of First USA earned tremendous returns on the stock while First USA was a public company, and then even greater returns as part of the merger. There were generous employee stock purchase plans at First USA so many employees had stock as well as stock options. Financially, shareholders and employees alike benefited from the growth story at First USA.

Today, First USA is the division that issues Chase credit cards. But those of us lucky enough to have been part of their unprecedented growth story saw firsthand the power of highly effective customer acquisition coupled with powerful customer retention.

Promotion-based Customer Acquisition

It's not just <u>who</u> you acquire as new customers that determines their LTV. <u>How</u> you acquire new customers can also lead to a lack of loyalty among your customer base.

First USA Bank is a good example of this. First USA was the first bankcard issuer to offer low introductory interest or 'teaser' rates to consumers with competitor cards. They offered new cardmembers the opportunity to transfer the balance on their current credit card to First USA and receive a much lower interest rate during a defined timeframe. Ultimately, this highly successful strategy was copied by every other bank.

While very effective for acquiring new cardmembers, in terms of ongoing customer loyalty, the introductory rate presented significant challenges.

First USA developed a powerful new offer to attract new customers and provided them a seamless process to leave their existing banks and move card balances to receive a much lower interest rate – for a while, that is. Those low 'teaser' rates remained in effect for a fixed number of months – typically 6 months at that time. As the introductory months ended – and competing banks began catching up in regard to replicating the offer – what First USA developed was a customer base they had 'trained' in regard to how easy it was to switch bankcard providers.

Customers Ready to Leave Your Brand

To be clear, I am among the first marketers to be an advocate for aggressive, promotion-based new customer acquisition and have worked with many brands to develop and implement these strategies. But, as we know, the most successful brand growth stories involve both growing customer acquisition and maximizing it with improved customer retention.

One of the points always proved by customer data is this: on average, if a group of customers are acquired using a special offer, they are more likely to attrite than customers acquired without the offer. Taking the special offer indicates a propensity to be persuaded by offers which – again, on average – means they have a higher chance of being captured by a competitor using promotional offers.

Examples of this exist in most industries. Subscription services often provide new customers introductory periods with no or reduced cost pricing to switch to their service. This is common in telecom, fitness memberships, internet services, subscription TV services, and more. Many retailers offer deep discounts during short purchase windows to entice new customers to experience their product. The examples most consumers encounter on a regular basis are vast.

Understanding the Customer Lifecycle

So, what do you do if you believe your customers, or segments of them, are not particularly loyal to your brand? The same thing you do with all customer retention strategy development. Start with analysis to understand the customer lifecycle with your brand.

When using promotions to attract new customers, the difficult second transaction may become even more difficult. Benchmark customers acquired with and without a promotion. If there are changes in the lifecycle for promotion customers, modify retention strategy to accommodate.

When using promotional offers with subscription-based businesses such as rent-to-own, utilities, fitness centers, and other businesses, you track customers from their initial sign-up into subsequent months. Barring contracts which 'require' customers to stay or a unique product markedly better than competitors, what you will see is a higher percentage of customers leave during the months which coincide with the end of the initial offer. What you will also likely see is that if you can 'manage customers' through this high attrition period you have a significantly higher chance of keeping them long term.

By now you should know the drill. You identify a group of customers that started doing business with you during a particular timeframe – typically twelve months earlier. Take all customers who started during a particular month. You then quantify the percentage of customers that end their relationship with you during each subsequent month over the course of their first year.

Once you understand the lifecycle of your customer segments, you may find you need to enhance the experience for certain segments at key times in that lifecycle. You would test into these strategies using test and control groups.

HOW TO SUCCEED

During the last twenty years, I have read many books about loyalty marketing. Most of them are interesting and provide insight on the topic. Many focus on attributes such as satisfaction, net promoter scores, and other engagement metrics, which are important barometers, for sure. But I found there was not a clear roadmap for how to apply what I had read to begin making a material change for a brand. Understanding the importance of select metrics was not a roadmap for materially changing the metric – nor was it clear that in all cases changes in metrics alone lead to the dramatic revenue growth which owners and Wall Street use as their ultimate measure of success.

My hope is that by reading this book you have taken another step toward advancing your professional career. Toward this we wrap up with a case study, examine additional considerations, and recap your road to success.

Case study: Specialty Retailer

A former colleague approached me to lead a loyalty assessment project with a school uniform company that had been in business for decades. During the prior decade there had been significant growth in the number of both private and charter schools across the US, and most of those require students to wear standardized clothing.

This rapid growth led to a number of new clothing providers entering the school uniform market. Catalogue clothing giant Land's End created a division to specifically source and market school uniforms. Manufacturers such as Tommy Hilfiger similarly followed suit. These large new market entrants made expanding the business difficult and the client was looking for ways to grow revenue.

Much of this industry approaches selling their products in two steps. The first is business-to-business (B2B) selling, where outside sales representatives call on schools to become an 'official' provider of school clothing to students. While some articles of clothing are branded with the school's name or crest, many of the required clothing options such as khaki shorts, pants, pullover polos, skirts, and similar items are available at a wide range of options, including discount retailers such as Walmart, Target, and Old Navy.

The uniform companies use a business-to-business selling technique that includes revenue-sharing back to the school to influence the school administration to do business with them. This means the clothing providers give back a percentage of revenue from the school's clothing sales to fund projects for the students. For example, 5% of gross sales for the year may be shared back at the end of a school year. To support this, the uniform company's retail and online sales track customers by name, address, and the school the children attend.

This model provides an advantage versus traditional brick-and-mortar retail stores without structured programs, where tracking individual customer behavior can be more difficult. For this provider of school uniforms, customers readily share their information when purchasing because they understand a percentage of sales is going back to support their children's schools.

This provided a tremendous untapped asset for a company relying heavily on traditional brick-and-mortar retail stores – robust customer-level tracking data. Since the people running the company had not read this book at the time (to be fair, the book did not exist at the time), they faced the same dilemma many companies face: Where does one start to grow a legacy business which has decreasing year-over-year revenue growth?

Step 1 – Business to Business sales

B2B sales organizations often rely heavily on an outside sales representative model to sign up new business entities and drive growth. These representatives are also typically responsible for maintaining relationships with the highest-revenue customers in their regions to retain them over time and, where possible, grow sales. Client sales representatives encouraged school administrators at high-revenue schools to promote their school clothing brand.

Revenue was tracked by school. Schools were then segmented based on total revenue generated and placed into traditional value tiers such as Platinum, Gold, Silver, and Bronze. Outside sales representatives were then assigned the small number of Platinum schools to actively 'manage'.

A deep dive into the model reveals growth opportunities

Time and resource constraints for outside sales representatives resulted in a small number of the high-revenue schools being proactively supported. Additionally, representatives depended on the school administrators themselves to execute 'marketing' for the uniform provider, including activities such as sending emails to parents on their behalf. While the administrators supported the uniform provider, they were understandably consumed with their primary goal of providing a quality education in a safe environment for their students.

If customer level data exists, it is always the place to start

The company had a tremendous untapped asset – their customer-level data.

Running a concentration of revenue and customer attrition analysis revealed what we see in many businesses:

1. A small percentage of customers drive a large portion of total brand revenue
2. Even good customers migrate to other providers over time if they are not engaged with both rational and emotional reasons to stay loyal to a brand.

We demonstrated to the client that their customers could also be placed into value tiers such as Platinum,

Gold, Silver and Bronze. As it turned out, the highest-revenue Platinum schools had one simple attribute that resulted in higher revenue than other schools. They had the highest student enrollments and therefore the most prospective customers for the school. The percentage of high-revenue customers was not materially different at these schools versus schools with lower enrollment and revenue. If 20% of a Platinum school's parents/guardians generated enough revenue to be considered 'best customers,' a similar percentage of customers existed at the smaller Gold, Silver, and Bronze schools.

Most schools – all not in the highest enrollment Platinum category - were not managed by sales representatives -- who simply did not have time to dedicate beyond their largest accounts.

We developed a B2B communications plan. While sales representatives could not physically visit or regularly call on the many schools in their region, with some administrative support from corporate they could send 'personalized' communications. Communications were developed to create at least the illusion of personalized, white-glove treatment and reinforce two key elements:

1. The reasons the school originally chose to do business with the uniform company
2. The initiatives the school could take to increase their revenue share from the uniform company by increasing sales to parents.

Effective business-to-business marketing would set a strong foundation. But this alone would not achieve the company's goals.

One-to-one focus on customers

The school uniform company's customer data coupled with quantitative research with customers lead to an effective strategy. Materially changing brand revenue trends required focus on the end-customers – parents and guardians purchasing clothing for students. Specifically, developing relationships with both high-revenue potential new customers and existing high-revenue customers and maintaining these relationships over time. This could be achieved by developing segmented 1-to-1 marketing using direct-to-consumer channels – in this case email, SMS, and in some instances traditional physical mail.

We also developed a customer loyalty program with clear benefits. The concept was designed to create the loss of tangible benefits for parents who chose to use other providers for initial school year purchases or replacement items during the year, and to provide rational reasons to continue shopping with the uniform company throughout the school year. Specifics included:

- Many customers purchased clothing during the busy back-to-school period but did not return during the year. Research indicated these parents used other clothing providers. Rebate benefits based on the amount of purchases during the back-to-school period would be used as rewards for enrolling in the program. These benefits were designed specifically to bring back customers during the important winter and spring shopping seasons.
- Customized member-only discounts would be offered to program members during non-peak

shopping seasons to stimulate purchase of cold-weather and spring seasonal items.
- Highest-value customers would receive additional benefits including free shipping and special member-only back-to-school shopping hours, allowing them to avoid crowds

The goal was engineering benefits to drive behaviors that increased revenue by creating passionately loyal customers. Data provided the roadmap to achieve this goal.

Working with consultants to develop loyalty strategy

During the last twenty years, all industries have grown to understand the power of effective CRM to grow revenue. This led to the creation of many client-service companies specializing in the marketing discipline.

When I joined Brierley + Partners, we used a program design methodology that engineered custom solutions appropriate for each unique brand and industry. But over the years, as the popularity of loyalty programs grew, and the number of loyalty focused firms increased, designers often based their design on what others were doing or what they liked best in the programs in which they participated.

Many data management companies who support these programs today have built points engines and standardized features which they offer to clients on an ongoing basis. After covering the cost of building their IT system, the profit margins from ongoing service fees can be tremendous, thus limiting a desire to customize a program to make it the most effective solution for each client.

The challenge this creates is that client service companies may perform strategy development services knowing full well what their final recommendations are going to be. Clients receive a recommended solution that utilizes the client service company's ongoing IT processing and related ongoing fees. For most clients, it does not make sense to build these capabilities internally. In some cases, however, points and other structured rewards just do not make sense. And even if they do, additional engagement benefits are necessary.

There are some tremendously talented companies offering valuable services, but much due diligence should be done when choosing a partner to develop effective loyalty strategy.

To succeed you need the right team

My experience at Brierley + Partners taught me one point in particular about launching major new customer initiatives. In order to succeed you need to bring in the right team early in the process.

You will need representation from all disciplines necessary for the project. This will vary depending on the brand but typically means representation from customer analytics, research, finance, marketing, field leadership, customer service and meeting with key stakeholders and senior leaders to understand their objectives from a new customer initiative.

While you may perform initial analysis to determine the revenue opportunity of the project, bringing in key stakeholders from across the organization early in the process will help ensure success.

Changing Paradigms

It is typically much easier to travel the well-traveled road when it comes to marketing strategy. Why not? It may be highly traveled because it works.

But there may be a better way.

Virgin America

As I said at the beginning of this book, in 2007 I joined the start-up leadership team at Virgin America.

By this point it had been over 25 years since American Airlines launched AAdvantage. From 1990 to 2007 alone there had been dozens of new airline startups across North America. Conceptually, every one of their loyalty programs followed the same model American used in 1981.

While the airline programs had proven to be hugely successful, there were inherent shortcomings in their designs.

For decades, the basic design included the following fundamentals:

Key design element 1

When flying with the sponsoring carrier, passengers earned miles based on how far they flew.

Economic Challenge: Two passengers sitting side by side on the same flight. One may have spent $1,000 for a roundtrip ticket and one $300. The roundtrip is 3,000 miles. In this model each passenger accrues the same miles despite their value to the carrier being drastically different.

Key design element 2

When it came to free flight redemption, free flight awards were set at fixed levels.

Consumer Challenge: For the same 25,000 miles, a passenger can 'buy' a free trip from Houston to Austin or from Houston to Boston -- despite the fact that the consumers' price for these trips is significantly different.

During my interview process, Virgin America shared very little regarding plans for the airline or loyalty program. Both Southwest Airlines and United Airlines have significant hubs in the San Francisco market and established airlines do not want to compete against new entrants. For example, whenever we announced Virgin America was going to serve a new destination from SFO, these carriers increased their flight frequency in the market and began double or triple earning incentives in their loyalty programs to reduce our opportunities for success.

From the interviews, I was aware Virgin planned to launch a program called Elevate – but that's all. I assumed the program would be another miles-based program based simply on the fact that both legacy and new entrant airlines had done this for decades.

A Nice Surprise

During my first day with Virgin America, I realized that while they had a program name, the design of the program had not been finalized, and with this revelation our path began to come into focus.

We designed a program structured to allow us to build both an emotional and rational connection with members. The program would award credit based on revenue – not miles flown. Passengers who spent more on tickets earned more credit.

We would buck the industry practice of blacking-out select seats, flights and days for redeeming awards. If there was a seat available on our plane, members could redeem a free flight. The program would have variable redemption rates for each award seat. The variable rates would not just be based on destination, but also on the day of week and time of day. For example, if an Elevate member living in San Francisco wanted an award seat to Las Vegas for the weekend, they could leave on a Friday when flights would typically be full or Saturday morning when seats were more readily available. The points required for each flight would be different – but fair – and members could decide if they wanted to wait until Saturday and use fewer points. The points needed for award seats were fair and, most importantly, rational.

We began flying on August 8, 2007 and had an immediate competitive advantage over every competing airline.

By 2011 both Jet Blue and Southwest airlines had copied our program structure exactly. As I write this now, most US legacy airlines have changed or are working toward changes in their programs to copy the program we launched as a small start-up.

Should you always seek to change the paradigm?

No. The answer is not always a better mousetrap.

At La Quinta Inn & Suites, the competitive review revealed LQ's program was both competitive and had the levers necessary to accomplish our objectives. The problem was how the program was managed – a common problem for many companies with structured customer programs. In the span of a few short years we went from a starting point of worst performance metrics in the industry to the highest metrics in the industry. We accomplished this without significant structural changes to the program. For any company this equation is true: *Customer engagement = brand growth.*

At La Quinta we took the equation a step further: *Customer engagement + Customer-facing employee engagement = Explosive growth.*

Make your partners part of the team

Having spent a considerable portion of my career as a consultant, I feel I have a good understanding of what it takes for client service resources to support clients. Corporate employees typically have not had these experiences and may view their resources as the 'paid help'.

That dynamic is just crazy.

It may be perpetuated by the first thing most private equity firms do when purchasing a company they plan to flip: they begin working on trimming costs and employees. Employees are often let go in favor of client service provider resources. The private equity firms assume that if they can optimize and sell the business, the most likely buyer will be a player in the same industry. This creates redundancies in personnel in the corporate departments.

To save the new company the uncomfortable work that comes with layoffs, they handle part of the job.

The client service resources are viewed differently from employees. They are simply let go when the time is right. Truth be known, client service employee jobs are typically fully funded by the client's work. And when the client work is stopped, these employees are often let go but the hands of the new owners don't get dirtied in this process.

But the point is you should treat your external partner resources at least as well as your own. These teammates are typically just as critical to a company's success as the internal team, and, with highly specialized skills, often even more so. They are your team members - with responsibilities for the success, or failure, of your efforts.

When my teams have success, we share and celebrate that success with the extended team. This fosters a bond that leads to increased commitment from all team members, internal or external.

Celebrate wins, even the small ones

It's important to keep everyone on the team engaged. Many companies have formal awards to recognize employee achievement. Achievement awards such as merit awards or Employee of the Year can be wonderful things. Our customer marketing team at La Quinta won an 'Employee of the Year' award at La Quinta's international conference. We were told it was the first time in company history that the award had been given to a team, not an individual. We celebrated the win with our external partner teams when we returned to our home city. The award was for the team and for us that meant the entire team.

But formal awards often, and rightfully, have bureaucracy attached or an agenda. They also may be awarded at specific times in a scheduled and expected manner.

As important as it is to engage the customer-facing employees, it is also important to motivate and engage both the internal and external project team members. The process to develop and execute strategies that allow a challenged brand to turn the corner are not glamorous.

At La Quinta, the Employee of the Month program we started within the customer marketing team was unlike any EOM award, or award process, that had ever preceded it.

We bought EOM plaques and inserted the funniest pictures we could find of winners (be careful what you put on Facebook!). We did not present the award monthly. Six or nine months might pass between awards and winners were nominated by other team members privately for their outstanding work. The first three winners were not even part of the internal team -- they were members of two of our client service partners.

As an add-on when the first award was presented, we made one of the rewards the use of our partner company president's office for a day. To make that more fun, we sent some posters to help transform this office into one perfect for the winner. This element took on more life over time as various comical props were used to highlight the winner's personality.

Margie was an important part of the internal LQ team. She was the last to win the award during my time at LQ. One of my team members quickly took on the job of rallying the team for ideas of what to do with my office while she used it.

While she had grown up in the United States, Margie was born in Poland. So, after some collaboration a theme was chosen – Margie would work in Poland. With that the office I typically used was transformed one evening into Poland, complete with snow, a chair fit for a queen, and images which celebrated Poland's heritage. It was so compelling that Margie worked in Poland for the entire week while I worked at her desk. Employees from all over the company stopped by to visit Poland. Here are a few pictures from this celebration.

CUSTOMER DEVOTION

Margie works in Poland

Margie being honored by the President of Poland

CUSTOMER DEVOTION

Celebrating a Polish Festival

Working in Poland

Make Loyalty a Company Pillar

Placing the appropriate weight on customer loyalty is critical. The title of the individual leading these efforts can speak volumes to employees at every level.

Case for why Loyalty should be a marketing pillar:

Customers are often the sole source of revenue. Staying close to them has never been more important.

Research/analytics have proven that only very satisfied AND engaged customers remain loyal.

Leading companies seek to build a strong base of loyal, profitable customers who also become advocates for the company.

For decades, companies have been making massive investments in CRM and customer-focused programs. These programs have continually raised the bar of customer experiences, making differentiation/impact in the marketplace difficult.

Customers' expectations continue to rise based on their collective experiences with other businesses. "Good enough" is no longer good enough.

Forward-thinking companies are building and managing customer advocates. Advocates are superior customers who spend more, stay loyal to the brand longer, and **refer others** - thus increasing both the quality of new customer acquisitions and, therefore, the overall customer base.

Titles beginning to be used include:

- Chief Loyalty Officer
- Chief Customer Officer
- Chief Customer Experience Officer

'Senior' is interchangeable with Chief in these examples and titles for each level within the customer marketing team should be considered.

Desired outcome:

The title emphasizes a company's recognition of and commitment to the role that **Customer Loyalty** plays in the long-term success of the brand. Employees in non-marketing disciplines, including customer-facing, will take notice. This reinforces a brand's commitment to building meaningful customer relationships.

What about customer fees?

As a creator of - and advocate for - Customer Devotion, it is not going to come as a surprise that in general I am not in favor of customer fees. Fees are used in many industries and, in some cases, with valid justification. Travel providers charge fees for cancelations or changes. Banks have fees for many items, including overdrafts, late payments, and on and on. Fees are prevalent with utilities services, travel, and many other industries. While a fee may be justified, the amount of the fee can cause tremendous dissatisfaction. Anyone who has paid an airline's $200 change fee understands this.

Customers do not like fees and therefore may leave your brand for a competitor after paying them. So why does a business implement fees? Plain and simple: because all or most of these fees go directly to the bottom line. Increasing fee revenue can be addicting as it pumps up profitability in the short term with little or no work from the organization. Once a company starts down a fee revenue path, the journey to drive more of this revenue may get treacherous over time.

While I hate customer fees, I LOVE growing revenue and profitability for a brand. So, in that respect, I understand why using fees to increase revenue remains pervasive. The challenge this creates is that over time there is a correlation between increasing customer fees and customer attrition. The correlation between these variables will become stronger over time.

Well-run organizations often 'test' raising fees with large groups of statistically relevant customers. As the individual responsible for Customer Devotion, I monitor and analyze these tests. The problem is that in many instances customers will withstand the fees, or fee increase, for some period of time. They may pay the higher or additional fee the first time and perhaps the second. Over time, however, fees are like small bits of poison for the relationship with your cherished customers — those same ones paying all the company's bills by purchasing your core services – and they start leaving. Then, you do not just lose the fee revenue, you lose ALL the revenue.

That said, fees may make sense for the organization. If all major competitors are charging the same type of fee(s) you may have more leeway. If the service is outside the norm of standard operations or there is additional cost to the company to perform it, there can be justification for fair and rational customer fees.

However, if you are offering your goods or services in a manner where consumers have clear pain points, a provider will move in that removes the customer pain points to compete more effectively.

For example, when Netflix first launched, it took on industry giant Blockbuster with the promise of "no late fees." The Netflix model initially mailed DVDs to customers who could return them whenever they wanted for a fixed monthly fee. Blockbuster charged by the rental and also charged steep late fees when rentals were not returned in time. And the success of Amazon Prime reflects consumers' desire to eliminate shipping fees.

But in some industries, fees are a way of life.

This exchange from Season 1 Episode 4 of Portlandia, during a cellphone purchase, comically illustrates fees:

"There is a nominal fee if you want to keep your current phone number."- Salesperson.

"I thought that was a free service." - Carrie.

"After you pay for it - it is free." - Salesman.

"Oh...Ok." - Fred.

"It's just a one-time fee...that you pay annually." - Salesperson.

"That's not a one-time fee..." - Fred.

"It is one-time in that you only pay one-time a year." - Salesperson.

Monitoring the impact of fees on retention – and designing appropriate communications when they occur -- will impact your success.

What is better than fees? In most industries it is providing product alternatives with varying degrees of 'value' and cost so that customers can purchase up or down the value chain to drive revenue in a positive, value-oriented way. This builds, not destroys, Customer Devotion.

Win by doing the right thing for customers

It sounds simple enough. Give customers a good product or service at a fair price and earn their continued business. This is a simple logic-driven principle, but as many companies begin to mature, the challenge of continued revenue growth may lead to decisions about customers which are short-sighted.

Sage Telecom was one of two new local telephone service entrants that were successful when local phone service was deregulated in 1996. They went up against the giant incumbent and carved out a significant percentage of market share.

They did it by launching something that was not offered at the time. They were leasing the phone lines from AT&T

at a wholesale rate, but those rates did not allow them to compete with significant margin against AT&T for basic phone service. For years, AT&T and the other monopolies made tremendous revenue from long-distance and add-on services like call waiting, voicemail, and other services. These were set up as separate business units with their own P/Ls to maximize the revenue of each individual component.

Sage launched a bundled set of local phone services at a rate for the bundle, which was in most cases cheaper than AT&T.

Sage was wildly successful, for a while. Many new companies entered this former monopolized space. AT&T was forced to improve both their service and marketing in order to retain customers who were defecting in significant numbers during the late 1990s and early 2000s.

When I joined Sage, we built analytic tools to track customer behavior. Sage had been successful for nearly a decade at that point, offering one product bundle to acquire and keep customers. They bundled local phone service, 250 minutes of free long-distance minutes each month, and several calling features such as call waiting, caller ID, and call forwarding.

As the environment got especially competitive, we dug deeply into customer behavior.

We analyzed the attributes of customers who started with Sage and stayed for the long haul versus those who tended to attrite early in their lifecycle.

What we found was that long-distance usage of customers was the #1 indicator of customer attrition. If they had low long-distance usage, say 100 minutes a month or less, they were at a much higher risk of attrition. If they had high long-distance usage, say 400 or more minutes a month, again they had a much higher likelihood of dropping our service. While Sage collected more revenue from the additional long-distance usage, these customers were simply not the right fit for the product we offered at the time.

In response to this analysis, we developed three different product bundles. A lower-cost basic plan, a moderate priced plan, and a more expensive plan with unlimited long-distance minutes.

Luckily for our team, the company was run by entrepreneurs who saw and took advantage of an opportunity when the government de-monopolized local phone service. They were not telecom industry executives. One challenge was that the margin on paid long-distance minutes was wildly profitable. Another was that a basic plan would sell at a lower margin than the current product bundle being sold.

We proposed a test. Take a group of customers who did not seem well-suited for their current plan bundle. Contact them through mail, and then follow up with a personal call for those that did not respond to the mail. Proactively offer customers the opportunity to **lower** their phone bill.

Many customers changed plans and saved money. Others who did not switch bundles still took notice of the fact that we proactively were trying to take care of them. This type of action was unheard of in telecom at the time (and remains largely true today).

Our risk was LOWER revenue from customers. You can guess what happened. Tracking customers we proactively reached out to versus identical customers we did not reach out to showed significantly lower attrition among the test group. Over time, we more than made up for the lost monthly revenue with customers who subscribed to our service for a longer period of time. We also built trust, and our customers began simply ignoring the offers of free months of service to come back to AT&T or switch to Comcast, Time Warner, or the many new companies offering local service.

The complete Sage Telecom story

Doing right by your customers makes them more loyal, even if it means lowering their costs and with it your own revenue. Sounds simple enough. Try proposing this to the CFO or your company. If done in the context of a well measured and controlled test – you have a chance.

Before I left my consulting position to join Sage I was in a meeting with AT&T management. Rumor had it that over the years they had hired nine different consultancies to help them develop structured loyalty strategies and were in the process of hiring the tenth. It would be years before they attempted their first effort.

At Sage Telecom we developed, tested, and rolled out the first structured customer loyalty program in telecom.

With an entrepreneurial team we accomplished this within eight months.

Fully understanding a brand's opportunity

Most companies measure topline revenue and customer growth. Achieving a moderate growth goal typically leaves them content.

For a typical consumer brand, segmented customer analysis will often reveal something like this: 50% of customers declined in year-over-year spend. 35% of customers stayed the same. 15% of customers grew spending – some of them by a tremendous amount. The net result may be that the group of customers with increasing revenue compensated for the declining customers and allowed the brand to achieve a growth goal – say growth of 5%-10%. For a mature business, this may satisfy ownership.

So, the question becomes: What if?

What if a portion of the declining customers didn't decline? What if they spent as much or more money year over year? In the consumer brand illustration just noted, a full 50% of customers declined in revenue year over year. That dynamic is not at all unusual.

What if a portion of the customers who were about the same, actually grew?

The answer to those questions is simple. Total company revenue no longer grows by a modest 5-10% a year. The company begins enjoying double-digit growth, the kind of growth that indicates actual Customer Devotion. Growth that results in investors with significantly enhanced returns, employees with higher salary increases each year, improved employee bonuses, and, for public companies, a growing stock price. Another added bonus – employees at every level are happy. And happy customer-facing employees lead to – you guessed it – happier customers.

How can I make those assessments? I have been through this change with a number of brands. Brands growing at modest rates – or even shrinking is some cases. As we achieved success, the overall culture changed. It's simply a lot more fun to work in an environment of success. And if celebrated across the organization, the feeling permeates every level of employee.

So, to review

What is necessary for CRM to be effective?

A successful loyalty initiative relies on these things being true.

1. Your customers are "splitting" their purchases among multiple providers
2. Additional highly relevant communications and incentives can encourage additional purchases with your brand

If these are true for a segment of customers, CRM has tremendous opportunity.

For most industries the conservative assumption for modeling incremental revenue opportunity is that members will not buy more of the goods or services. Incremental revenue is generated when program members consolidate purchases with the program's sponsor. Select industries however do have an opportunity for incremental purchases within the category – but modeling this into the economics should be done conservatively.

So how do you create a best in class successful program?

Don't take shortcuts.

Keys to Success

1. Start with understanding current customer behavior.
    - Customer level analysis will determine where a brand is 'winning' and where there are opportunities to improve. Key times for interventions to stimulate sales, save defecting customers and engage newer customers.
    - Understanding current buying behavior and motivations of current customers will help shape the most effective program

structure and communications to drive incremental share.
2. Qualitative research, followed by an e-based quantitative survey to current customers, could provide tremendous insight on opportunities to increase customer share and corresponding revenue.
3. Customer segmentation and communications which are engineered to have the right messages for the right customer segments at the right time(s) are required for the long-term success of a program.

A successful CRM effort will dramatically change the growth trend of any consumer brand.

The best defense is...defense

Many of you may have heard the adage that "the best defense is a good offense." While this principle may be advantageous in some sports and military exercises, it's not a mindset you want to consider when it comes to retaining your most profitable customers.

Retention begins with customer acquisition strategies. Effective brands develop strategies to target prospective long-term customers who have the following attributes:

- Characteristics consistent with current high-value customers, which indicates;
- High spending in the goods/service category offered by the brand

What that means is that <u>your</u> most profitable customers today, the very ones you consider to be most 'loyal', should be the #1 target for acquisition by <u>your competitors</u>.

They would do this by identifying high-value-potential characteristics for their new customers. Among most brands, even loyal customers occasionally make purchases with competing companies.

So, what you develop and implement is aggressive, differentiated, relevant marketing communications and focused benefits to keep that customer coming back to your brand.

For transactional businesses focus is on the two keys to long-term success:

1. Getting second transactions from new customers
2. Building wildly strong relationships with your most profitable customers

In short, your goal is 'defending' your highest revenue customers. You accomplish this by applying the principles covered in this book. Work to build real relationships with your best customers.

When one of your best customers transacts at a competitor for convenience, to try something new, or other reasons, and that competitor reaches out to drive their second transaction, you need to have shown these customers more 'love' than any other business in your category. If you have done that effectively, the competing brand's efforts will be far less effective.

The job of creating that relationship started the moment those high-value customers first interacted with your brand. Creating Customer Devotion means never taking these customers for granted. As they continue doing business with you, fewer of them will defect to competitors.

As customers become high-value, they should require fewer discounts and promotional offers to retain. However, you never stop recognizing these customers as your most important. Thank them for their business. Both communicate and demonstrate that you will take better care of them than any other provider.

Low Hanging Fruit

I love the 'low hanging fruit' comment I often hear when taking on a new challenge. The context is in regard to efforts which can be easily implemented to have a dramatic impact on revenue. Sure, there may be non-exploited tactics that can be implemented to drive additional revenue. But if the company has been around for a while, someone has usually done something with these 'low hanging' tactics along the way – and these alone typically do not dramatically change brand growth. Dramatic brand growth usually involves fruit higher on the tree.

Brand growth takes superior customer analytics that drive impactful marketing strategies that are then tested with valid measurement techniques. These strategies are then refined and expanded to increase customer LTVs and grow brands. Innovative strategies and marketing campaigns will emerge as part of the overall process.

While I so wish it were the case, I have yet to find a way to achieve dramatic results using short cuts.

The Brand Growth Unicorn – the 'Home Run'

Many senior marketing professionals praising the virtues of implementing growth strategies get focused on executing a single big idea, or message, that will – in theory at least – start growing brand revenue quickly. The proverbial Grand Slam Home Run.

Much energy can be put into swinging for the fences by developing and executing these overnight game changers. In my experience, there are few true 'home runs.' In decades of professional experience, working with dozens of brands large and small, I have seen this exactly once.

How most successful brands actually grow - 'Hitting Singles'

If you take away just one insight from this book, let it be this:

While you always want to be looking for the 'home run', if your brand does not begin to hit consistent singles, it will not achieve consistent measured success.

How to define Singles?

The teams I have worked with define singles as a measured step, to gain an actionable insight, which, when combined with other customer interactions, results in measured revenue growth. Just like in baseball, hit a few singles and you score a run. Keep working on the big ideas but stay dedicated to being deep in the data hitting singles. While others may be searching for the elusive home run, you hit 10, 15, 20 singles along the way scoring multiple runs -- each one driving revenue growth for the brand.

You hit singles using a methodology which includes the steps outlined in the book. If your path includes development of a customer facing program, follow a project plan that includes these steps:

MIKE CASE

Activity

Discovery

Project Kick-Off
- Conduct initial management or client interviews
- Identify stakeholders, business issues & desired outcomes
- Review project plan, timeline and milestone dates
- Finalize project goals and objectives

Review Customer Data & Prior Research as applicable
- Review prior research (as applicable)
- Develop specifications for customer data summary/extraction
- Review past customer purchase behavior; Potential segmentation strategies
- Assess current customer value

Review Brand Assets & Marketing Initiatives
- Review currently identified brand assets that may be leveraged
- Review current database marketing initiatives and promotions

Consumer Research / Program Design Input

Qualitative Research
- Develop research plan/identify research audience and 'segments'
- Develop focus group/interview guide and questions
- Conduct customer interviews
- Summarize/report of research results

Quantitative Research
- Develop research plan/identify research audience and 'segments'
- Develop research questionnaire
- Launch surveys
- Report of research results

Ideation & Program Design

Preliminary Program Design
- Conduct ideation brainstorming sessions with employees and stakeholders
- Identify potential program benefits, rewards, value proposition alternatives
- Identify opportunities, if available to leverage brand partners or sponsors
- Identify alternative program reward offerings/value propositions

Program Design Enhancements
- Evaluate alternative program reward offerings/value propositions
- Determine optimal reward structure and mix of relationship tools

Creative Development

Develop Program Positioning, Name, Graphic Approach

Business Modeling & Program Recommendations

Determine Operations Infrastructure to Support Program
- Outline technical issues/systems requirements to support program
- Assess current brand systems capabilities, recommend enhancements as required
- Develop timeline for implementation of technology infrastructure as/if required

Develop Financial 'Business Case'
- Assess opportunity
- Estimate program revenue/operating costs for 1st year rollout; ongoing
- Define operating budget
- Identify success metrics

Develop Implementation Plan
- Develop implementation/(test as applicable) plan
- Develop launch/exit strategy

Final Business Case, Program Recommendations & Implementation Plan

Implementation / Pilot Test

As it turns out...

Even in Major League Baseball the majority of runs are not the result of home runs. Most runs are batted in after runners reached base on, you guessed it, singles.

Corporate America doesn't want to believe

A few years back I was invited to an executive roundtable with management from a wide range of brands to discuss customer loyalty. Several members of the AT&T executive team at the time attended this meeting. Twenty individuals were invited to facilitate discussion and sharing of ideas. The AT&T executives were talking about the challenges they faced at the time. It had been years since Sage Telecom had been sold and the marketing strategies we launched had been sent to thousands of customers, so the execution strategies were publicly available.

These AT&T executives were familiar with Sage as we had been a small but impactful threat to them before we sold the business. I explained the techniques we used to have such a profound impact on our customers to create such passionate loyalty. The AT&T executives looked me right in the eyes and told me "there is no way that could have had such a powerful impact." These were executives with dozens of years of experience – unfortunately their experience was at a large corporation with an old school mindset. I refrained from asking them how it went with the tenth company AT&T hired to help them with customer loyalty.

There was no reason to argue the point. The former management, marketing, and customer service teams from Sage all well know the profound impact we had on our customers.

It's not easy to drive customer preference and create advocates in low-engagement categories. But to the belief it cannot be done in dramatic fashion, I offer this:

> *A small marketing team working in close concert with an engaged customer-facing organization drove wildly enthusiastic engagement in a traditionally low-engagement category: local telephone service. The result - a dramatically more valuable organization.*

EPILOGUE

It's time to get started. You have the tools and analytic strategies to begin the journey of dramatically growing your brand. As I have noted this journey is neither short nor easy. But the destination is tremendously rewarding.

If you need assistance achieving your goals I am here to help. This can range from talking to management about the virtues of the Customer Devotion journey, planning an approach to achieve your goals, executing strategic analysis or implementing marketing strategies that work.

Feel free to visit www.customerdevotion.com or reach out to me directly at mikecase@customerdevotion.com. Here's to your success.

ABOUT THE AUTHOR

Mike Case is a recognized and award-winning leader with decades of experience leading successful, comprehensive marketing efforts to dramatically grow brands.

Mike's work with the La Quinta Returns® loyalty program resulted in a full doubling of all guest loyalty metrics, including doubling loyalty member total brand revenue. These gains fueled dramatic brand growth and facilitated a successful IPO. Prior to La Quinta, Mike led the development and launch of the game-changing loyalty program for Virgin America – the first-ever U.S. airline loyalty program based on passenger revenue rather than miles flown. Additionally, he developed and implemented transformative customer loyalty initiatives for brands across other industries such as Sage Telecom, and built product enhancements to support the launch of the first Visa Platinum bankcard (First USA). Mike's work is at the forefront of industry-recognized, breakthrough marketing strategies.

A highly sought-after speaker Mike has been invited to conferences including Colloquy's Customer Experience

Conference and the Epsilon Symposium. He has presented to top MBA programs including University of Chicago Booth School of Business and Southern Methodist University's Cox school.

Visit **www.customerdevotion.com** to learn more about creating true customer devotion.

Made in the USA
Coppell, TX
21 January 2025

44750194R00105